THE CHINESE MASSACRE (ANNOTATED)

Tom Jacobson

BROADWAY PLAY PUBLISHING INC
New York
www.broadwayplaypublishing.com
info@broadwayplaypublishing.com

First printing: March 2013
I S B N: 978-0-88145-555-7

Book design: Marie Donovan
Page make-up: Adobe Indesign
Typeface: Palatino
Printed and bound in the U S A

THE CHINESE MASSACRE (ANNOTATED) had
its world premiere by Circle X Theatre Company at
Atwater Village Theatre, Los Angeles on 22 April 2011.
The cast and creative contributors were:

Richard Azurdia—JESUS BILDERRAIN, CRISTOBAL
AGUILAR, ESTEBAN SANCHEZ, ADOLFO CELIS, JESUS
MARTINEZ, ANNOTATOR

Warren Davis—JOHN TRAFFORD, HILLIARD
LOWENSTEIN, JAMES BURNS, LOUIS MENDEL

Anna Douglas—LYDIA SCHUBERT, SISTER RASINDA,
ANN CAROL, ROSARIO THOMPSON, WHITE WOMAN IN
CROWD

Elizabeth Ho—YUT HO

Ross Kurt Le—AH CHOY, WONG TUCK, CHINESE MAN

Jully Lee—TONG YU, ANNOTATOR

Alex Levin—HENRY HAZARD, BENJAMIN MCLAUGHLIN,
ROBERT THOMPSON, GEORGE FALL

West Liang—LEE TONG, LEE

Johanna McKay—ROSA LOWENSTEIN, SISTER
PRUDENCIA, WHITE WOMAN IN CROWD, ANNOTATOR

Silas Wier Mitchell—REVEREND CRENSHAW, CURLY
CRENSHAW

Gary Patent—EUGENE MEYER, FRANK BAKER, CHARLES
AUSTIN

Jack Sochet—EMIL HARRIS, ANDREW JACKSON KING,
ALEXANDER JOHNSON

Lisa Tharps—BIDDY MASON, ANNOTATOR

Ryun Yu—GENE TONG, YO HING, SAM YUEN

Director ....Jeff Liu
Producers .... Tim Wright & Jennifer A Skinner
Associate producers .... Jen Kays & Camille Schenkkan
Stage manager....................................... Katherine E. Haan
Graphic design .... Rita Ikerd and Noah Scalin
Publicity... Lucy Pollak
Scenic design..................................... Sibyl Wickersheimer
Lighting design .... Thomas Ontiveros
Costume design.................................... Dianne K. Graebner
Sound design...................................... Dennis Yen
Dialect coach .... Tracy Winters
Properties .... Michael O'Hara

CHARACTERS & SETTING

LEE, *40, a Chinese physician, also plays*
  LEE TONG, *20, an herbalist's apprentice*

REVEREND CRENSHAW, *40, an American revivalist, also plays*
  CURLY CRENSHAW, *20, a teamster and groom*

YUT HO, *19, a beautiful Chinese woman*

GENE TONG, *26, a Chinese herbalist and* LEE TONG's *brother, also plays*
  YO HING, *35, head of the Hong Chow Company*
  SAM YUEN, *35, head of the Nin Yung Company*

JOHN TRAFFORD, *38, a Justice of the Peace from England, also plays*
  HILLIARD LOEWENSTEIN, *43, a Prussian dry goods merchant*
  JAMES BURNS, *39, American sheriff*
  LOUIS MENDEL, *40, a Prussian laborer*

EUGENE MEYER, *30, French dry goods merchant, also plays*
  FRANK BAKER, *42, city marshall*
  CHARLES AUSTIN, *30, former constable*

ANDREW JACKSON KING, *35, a newspaper editor from Georgia, also plays*
  EMIL HARRIS, *28, a Prussian policeman*
  ALEXANDER JOHNSON, *36, Irish bootmaker*

AH CHOY, 25, *a Chinese thug, also plays*
WONG TUCK, 25, *a Chinese cook*
CHINESE MAN

HENRY HAZARD, 27, *an attorney from Illinois, also plays*
ROBERT THOMPSON, 41, *a saloon keeper*
BENJAMIN MCLAUGHLIN, 35, *a witness*
GEORGE FALL, 28, *a newspaper editor*

LYDIA SCHUBERT, 18, *a Prussian girl, also plays*
ANN CAROL, 24, *an Irish house servant*
SISTER RASINDA, 30, *an Irish nun*
WHITE WOMAN IN CROWD
ROSARIO THOMPSON, 25, ROBERT'*s wife*

ROSA LOEWENSTEIN, 35, *wife of* HILLIARD LOEWENSTEIN,
also plays
WHITE WOMAN IN CROWD
SISTER PRUDENCIA, 30, *a Sister of Charity*

JESUS BILDERRAIN, 32, *a policeman from Mexico, also plays*
CRISTOBAL AGUILAR, 57, *California Mayor*
ESTEBAN SANCHEZ, 30, *a California policeman*
ADOLPHO CELIS, 20, *a California laborer*
JESUS MARTINEZ, 28, *a Mexican sexton*

BIDDY MASON, 54, *a midwife from Georgia, former slave*

TONG YU, 25, GENE TONG'*s wife*

*The action takes place in various locations throughout Los
Angeles in January 1891 and October 1871, including an
elegant but old adobe home, a courtroom, a bedroom, an
herbalist's office, a saloon, a dry goods store, the street, and
an underground tunnel.*

*Setting: Twelve chairs rearranged variously on three levels
through the play.*

NOTES & ACKNOWLEDGMENTS

Throughout the play are ANNOTATIONS, speeches spoken as asides by characters on stage at the director's discretion. Costume changes, as each actor becomes a different character, may be done in full view of the audience. In the riot sequences, the CROWD is never fully visible, but present in the darkness, heard but barely seen.

I am indebted to many for their assistance in the development of this play, including Circle X Theatre Company, the Los Angeles History Project, William Estrada, Betty Uyeda, Lisa Tang, John Cahoon, Phil Chung, Jeff Liu, Marshall Wong, Tim Wright, Camille Brown, Richard Azurdia, and Jen Kays.

ACT ONE

(Interior of an elegantly appointed parlor in Los Angeles in January 1891. REVEREND CRENSHAW, *40, well dressed, stands at the open door. Outside stands* LEE, *40, Chinese, dressed in American style.)*

LEE: *(American accent)* I understand you have an unusual item for sale. *(No response. He produces a clipping.)* The *Los Angeles Record.* January 16th, 1891.

ANNOTATION: *Los Angeles Record,* published 1889 to 1931.

REVEREND CRENSHAW: It's late.

LEE: Is it sold?

REVEREND CRENSHAW: Late at night.

LEE: My apologies, sir. I've just arrived from San Francisco. *(Consulting clipping)* Am I addressing L F Crenshaw?

REVEREND CRENSHAW: *(Leaving the door open, heading for a chair, limping slightly)* Reverend Crenshaw.

LEE: *(Following)* Oh. Of which faith?

REVEREND CRENSHAW: *(Sitting)* Christian.

LEE: I meant what denomination.

REVEREND CRENSHAW: Christian. And you are?

LEE: *(Sitting)* I possess neither faith nor denomination, sir.

REVEREND CRENSHAW: I meant your name.

LEE: *(Extending his hand)* My name is Lee.

(REVEREND CRENSHAW ignores it.)

LEE: Is the item still available?

REVEREND CRENSHAW: It's a rare curiosity.

LEE: That's my understanding.

REVEREND CRENSHAW: Of interest only to specialized collectors.

LEE: I am one such, sir. The advertisement intrigued me greatly.

ANNOTATION: For sale: Anatomical specimen. Preserved Chinese finger, right pinky. Historic interest. L F Crenshaw, Los Angeles.

REVEREND CRENSHAW: You'd like to buy my chinky finger.

LEE: Indeed. I could hardly expect you to give it to me. May I see it?

REVEREND CRENSHAW: *(Fetching the finger)* As much as I'd like to give you the finger, Mister Lee, I cannot. Please, have a seat.

(LEE, already seated, looks confused.)

ANNOTATION: In this annotated version of *The Chinese Massacre*, the action will be periodically interrupted by footnotes—like this one—intended not only to provide important background information and historic detail from original sources, but also to distance the audience from the emotionality of the story in the style of Bertolt Brecht's epic theatre. By reminding you constantly that you are watching a carefully edited story rather than actual history, the play demands that you experience it with your mind, not your heart.

REVEREND CRENSHAW: *(Returning with a small box)* And what payment are you offering, Mister Lee?

LEE: *(Reaching for the box)* I had thought ten dollars a fair price.

REVEREND CRENSHAW: *(Withdrawing the box)* Ten dollars?

ANNOTATION: When reading an essay most people skip the footnotes. Here, stuck in your theatre seat, you will endure them all.

LEE: A finger is of little use to anyone other than its original owner. Ten dollars strikes me as quite fair for something of negligible value.

REVEREND CRENSHAW: You are indeed of little faith, Mr. Lee. This withered flesh and brittle bone played a vital role in the history of the city of Los Angeles.

(REVEREND CRENSHAW opens the box and takes out a two-inch dried pinky finger, displaying it for LEE, but holding it away from him.)

ANNOTATION: In 1836 "El Pueblo de Nuestra Señora la Reina de Los Angeles" became the nominal capital of the Mexican province Alta California, and it was the last place to surrender to the United States at the time of the American occupation in 1847. According to the United States Census, the population of Los Angeles in 1890 was 50,395, ranking 57th in the nation.

LEE: It seems to me a perfectly ordinary dried finger.

REVEREND CRENSHAW: It's a chinky pinky. See how dark?

LEE: It could be anyone's. From anywhere. It could be a hundred years old, it could be a year.

REVEREND CRENSHAW: I know for a fact it's twenty years old. And exactly where it came from.

LEE: You can prove provenance?

REVEREND CRENSHAW: What's provenance?

LEE: Exactly where it came from.

REVEREND CRENSHAW: I said as much, did I not? It's worth far more than a scant ten dollars.

LEE: What will you charge, sir?

REVEREND CRENSHAW: Fifty dollars, Mister Lee, seems eminently reasonable.

LEE: Fifty! Surely a revival preacher of renown, so— *(Gestures to the handsomely appointed room)* —Blessed by the Almighty—has little concern for commerce.

REVEREND CRENSHAW: Quite right, sir. I am merely tired of the gruesome artifact. Why are you so avid to acquire it?

LEE: I knew I would be in town and thought I should inquire.

REVEREND CRENSHAW: And your business in Los Angeles, Mister Lee?

LEE: A funeral.

REVEREND CRENSHAW: Ah. My condolences. I pray the departed was a Christian soul not destined to scorch for all time.

LEE: Most certainly a Christian, Reverend. I am willing to bargain, but you've given me no surety of authenticity.

REVEREND CRENSHAW: Provenance.

LEE: Yes.

REVEREND CRENSHAW: That could well increase the price. I have a number of other prospective buyers.

LEE: I am a reasonable man, sir, with some resources. How did it come into your possession? Unattached human fingers are uncommon items—*chinky*—or no.

REVEREND CRENSHAW: I didn't detach it myself, if that's what you're implying.

LEE: Not at all.

REVEREND CRENSHAW: Everyone in Los Angeles knows the story.

LEE: I am from San Francisco, sir.

ANNOTATION: The 1890 population of San Francisco was 298,997 according to the U S Census.

REVEREND CRENSHAW: A tragic day, but justice was served despite the official graft that infected the city. Mind you, I wasn't there for most of it.

LEE: Your point of view will do, sir. What day?

REVEREND CRENSHAW: October 24th, 1871.

ANNOTATION: The 1870 population of Los Angeles was 5,728 according to the U.S. Census.

(Lights begin to dim on REVEREND CRENSHAW *and* LEE *and come up on* JUSTICE JOHN TRAFFORD, *38, and* ANDREW JACKSON KING, *35, a newspaper editor and attorney.)*

REVEREND CRENSHAW: And like many tragedies, it began with a marriage.

TRAFFORD: *(English accent)* I'm not at all certain this is legal.

REVEREND CRENSHAW: Four days earlier, October 20, 1871.

(Lights out completely on REVEREND CRENSHAW *and* LEE.)*

KING: *(Southern accent)* The city clerk signed the license.

TRAFFORD: They're Chinese, heathens.

KING: It's a civil ceremony, Justice. And they're sponsored by our friend Yo Hing.

TRAFFORD: Which company is he with? I can't keep track.

KING: The Hong Chow Company, the good one. He was my cook till he became a cigar maker, done well for himself. Practically American. *(Calling)* Yo!

TRAFFORD: These Mongolian girls don't get married— they're all prostitutes—

(YO HING, 35, a stocky man dressed in Chinese style, ushers in YUT HO, 19, a beautiful Chinese bride.)

KING: This one wants an American ceremony. She's a good girl, isn't she, Yo?

YO: *(Quiet and polite)* Good girl, yes, very good. And beautiful—see.

(YO displays YUT HO like merchandise.)

TRAFFORD: Is this the groom?

KING: This is Yo Hing.

YO: *(Bowing)* Mucho gusto!

TRAFFORD: *(Without much gusto)* Mucho gusto. Where is said groom?

YO: Groom?

KING: Husband.

YO: Husband. Come very quick. *(Calling)* Lay Tong guor gor lay! [Tong, get your ass in here!]

(LEE TONG, 20, dashes in. He is dressed in Chinese style, including a long queue.)

LEE TONG: Sorry late. *(Gestures to his wedding clothes)* I—change. *(To YUT HO)* Lay ho leng ah. [You look beautiful!]

YUT HO: *Nguor hi mm-woi tong lay geet fun gah. Nguor yee-qing gaw jo yaan lah.* [I'm not marrying you. I'm already married.]

YO: *Lay mm-high ga-jor lay. Lay high bay-migh jor lay!*
[You're not married—you were sold!]

LEE TONG: *Ngor-day gao lay!* [We're saving you!]

YO: So sorry, sir. Good girl, yes. We make marriage
now?

TRAFFORD: For God's sake, yes, let's get this over with.
Do you—what is his name?

KING, LEE TONG, YO: Tong.

ANNOTATION: In 1871
several American marriages
were performed—

TRAFFORD: Do you,
Tong, take—

ANNOTATION: As a way of
changing ownership—

YO: Yut Ho.

ANNOTATION: —Of Chinese
women from one company
to another. Often they were
kidnapped, as was Yut Ho.
She was previously married
to a much older Chinese
man from the Nin Yung
Company in a Chinese
ceremony. You would
already know that if you
spoke Cantonese.

TRAFFORD: Yut Ho as
your wife, from this day
forward, for better, for
worse, for richer, for
poorer, in sickness and
in health, to love, honor
and cherish her, keeping
yourself only unto her for
as long as you both shall
live? If so, answer "I do."

LEE TONG & YO: *(As YO nudges LEE TONG)* I do.

ANNOTATION: According to
the Los Angeles County
Registrar's Office, similar
legally binding American
marriages performed that
year were for Ah Chun and
Sy Ku, Ah Kit and Sung
Kum, Ah Sum and One Que,
and One Za and Sing Hee,

TRAFFORD: Do you, Yut
Ho, take Tong as your
husband, from this day
forward, for better, for
worse, for richer, for
poorer, in sickness and
in health, to love, honor
and cherish him, keeping
yourself only unto him

but our play presents this as the first for dramatic effect.

for as long as you both shall live? If so, answer "I do."

YO & YUT HO: *(As* YO *nudges* YUT HO*)* I do.

TRAFFORD: Are there...uh...rings?

YO: Very high price ring for very good girl.

*(*YO *produces two rings, slipping them onto* YUT HO *and* LEE TONG's *fingers.)*

YUT HO: *Gum, tong-mau geen-sek!* [Gold—and a diamond!]

TRAFFORD: Then I pronounce you man and wife. You may kiss the bride.

LEE TONG: *High gom-door yan meen-tching?* [In front of people?]

YO: *Sek kuoy!* [Kiss her!]

KING: Kiss her!

*(*YUT HO *visibly flinches when* LEE TONG *reaches for her, but she consents to the kiss. Just as their lips meet, a shot rings out. Everyone ducks for cover as* AH CHOY, *25, a Chinese thug, bursts into the room brandishing a pistol.* YO HING *returns fire.)*

AH CHOY: *Kuoy yee-king tong Sing Hing geet jor fan la wo!* [She's already married to Sing Hing!]

KING: Duck, Judge!

YO: *Gum yao deem ah?* [So what?]

TRAFFORD: King, you buffoon, you've got us in the middle of a tong war!

LEE TONG: *Lay fai-dee guor lay nguor lee-do!* [Stay behind me!]

KING: Help, officer! Somebody!

YUT HO: *Nguor mm-sigh yoo gua sigh-low lay bow-woo*

TRAFFORD: There's no officer!

nguor! [I don't need a boy
to protect me.]

ANNOTATION: In 1871, there were only six policemen in
the City of Los Angeles.

LEE TONG: *Nguor mm-high*   AH CHOY: *Sam Yuen*
sign-low, nguor high lay geh   *gee-dough lay seung de!*
nam-yan! [I'm not a boy,   [Sam Yuen knows what
I'm your husband!]   you're up to!]

(HENRY HAZARD, 27, *bursts into the room behind* AH
CHOY, *stopping the fight by putting a gun to* AH CHOY's
head.)

YO: *Nguor do goo-do lay-high*   HENRY: Hey, this is a
Sam-geh fai-lu! [I knew you   courthouse! Enough of
were Sam's tool!]   that!

HENRY: For the love of decency—!

KING: *(Coming out of hiding)* Thanks, officer.

HENRY: I'm not an officer, I'm an attorney!

(Everyone comes out of hiding.)

KING: Then what are you doing with a pistol?

HENRY: When I came from Illinois, they told me I'd
need one.

ANNOTATION: Early historians called Los Angeles
vice-ridden and corrupt, "undoubtedly the toughest
town in the nation, a staging place for drifters," with a
reputation that "did little to attract visitors".

TRAFFORD: Let's indict these two.

HENRY: Right now?

TRAFFORD: All interested parties are present.

HENRY: What about due process? What about a jury?

TRAFFORD: *(Waving away the objection)* Do you have the
chicken head?

HENRY: Chicken head?

KING: Being unchurched, the Chinese can't be expected to uphold an oath sworn on the Bible, so we use— (*Produces a severed chicken head*)

YO: Very sacred. Chinaman must tell truth.

HENRY: You've done this before.

TRAFFORD: They are a litigious people.

ANNOTATION: The chicken head or chicken blood oath was commonly used among Chinese immigrants in the American west.

TRAFFORD: (*To* YO *and* AH CHOY) Do you swear what you are about to speak is the truth, the whole truth, and nothing but the truth?

HENRY: (*Sotto voce*) So help you, chicken head?

AH CHOY & YO: (*Their hands over the chicken head*) I do.

TRAFFORD: (*To* LEE TONG *and* YUT HO) You may go. This doesn't concern you.

HENRY: Objection! They're witnesses!

KING: But they can't testify.

HENRY: Whyever not?

KING & TRAFFORD: It's the law.

HENRY: But you just swore in these two.

TRAFFORD: Only to plead.

(TRAFFORD *gestures, and* YUT HO *and* LEE TONG *leave.*)

ANNOTATION: In 1853 George Hall was tried for murder of a Chinese man but the verdict was overturned by the State Supreme Court—

TRAFFORD: You both stand accused of disturbing the peace with intent to cause bodily harm. How do you plead?

ANNOTATION: —Because the conviction was based on—

KING: Not guilty, your honor.

ANNOTATION: —Testimony by Chinese witnesses.

TRAFFORD: Bail is one thousand dollars. Counsel?

(YO bows to TRAFFORD. KING signs for the bail and leaves with YO.)

ANNOTATION: The chief justice ruled that—

HENRY: I'm not his counsel!

ANNOTATION: —Since Native Americans had originally come into North America across the Bering Strait—

TRAFFORD: I just appointed you. Not guilty? Thought so.

ANNOTATION: The 1850 Act prohibiting Indian testimony—

HENRY: I very much beg your pardon! Objection!

ANNOTATION: —"Extended to the whole of the Mongolian race."

TRAFFORD: Bail is set at one thousand dollars.

(HENRY is astonished. AH CHOY shrugs.)

ANNOTATION: The prohibition of Chinese testimony was written into the statute books ten years later.

HENRY: Well, I'm not signing for it.

ANNOTATION: California Statute 69, Act of March 18, 1863.

TRAFFORD: Then I have no choice but to remand your client to jail.

HENRY: He's not my client! This is ridiculous! You're making this up as you go along!

TRAFFORD: Frontier justice, counsel. You're not in Illinois any more.

(EMIL HARRIS, *28, a Prussian policeman, comes in with* SAM YUEN, *35, the head of the Nin Yung Company, dressed in American style, with no queue.*)

EMIL: *(German accent)* Excuse me, Judge. Sam Yuen would like a word with you.

SAM: *(Enthusiastic and excitable)* Me got bail! You settee Chinaman free?

ANNOTATION: You may have noticed by now that some actors in this play have taken on multiple roles. Not only does this conceit save money on actor stipends, it also heightens the theatricality of the alienation effect.

TRAFFORD: Sam, is this your man?

SAM: Him work Nin Yung Company. Good Chinaman!

(SAM *to* AH CHOY, *who returns the bow.*)

TRAFFORD: Bail is one thousand dollars.

SAM: Me have six thousand in Wing Chung store.

TRAFFORD: Now, Sam, how am I to believe you?

SAM: In gold!

TRAFFORD: I am most certainly unavailable to traipse over to Nigger Alley to verify your claim.

ANNOTATION: The street Calle de los Negros, so named during the Californio period because of the dark-skinned Mexican residents—

EMIL: Judge, Nigger Alley's in my beat. I can easily perambulate to that locality.

ANNOTATION: —By 1871 was populated almost entirely by the Chinese. English language maps—

(SAM *whispers to* EMIL.)

TRAFFORD: Very well. Prisoner is released to your custody.

ANNOTATION: —And newspapers translated the street name to the vernacular.

EMIL: Thank you, Judge. Sam Yuen has asked me to add that Yo Hing of the Hong Chow Company has perverted the machinery of law under the names of his various tools and creatures.

TRAFFORD: Perversion noted. Court adjourned. *(Pounds his gavel)* Counsel?

HENRY: *(Reluctantly)* Your Honor?

TRAFFORD: While I appreciate your quick draw, in general I'd advise you not to risk your own skin for these people.

HENRY: Your Honor—sir—justice demands—

TRAFFORD: Welcome to Los Angeles, Counsel. *(Pounds again)*

(Lights out on AH CHOY, EMIL, HENRY, SAM, *and* TRAFFORD. *Lights up on* LEE *and* REVEREND CRENSHAW *in 1891.)*

LEE: Reverend, I have difficulty believing the Chinese spoke in such a silly, childlike manner.

REVEREND CRENSHAW: Tis a childlike race, bereft of God's saving grace. I was there, sir. I know what I heard. If you have difficulty comprehending, kindly consult the newspaper archive.

ANNOTATION: A quote from Yo Hing as interviewed by the Los Angeles press:

YO: *(Appearing)* Chinaman very smart; heap stealee woman. Woman no likee be bad; woman she get married—bad Chinaman he likee sell woman. Police likee money—he heap catchee woman—big pay.

ANNOTATION: *Los Angeles News*, February 25th, 1872.

LEE: I have indeed consulted archives, Reverend, and remember Yo Hing's letters to the papers as highly articulate.

YO: Evil disposed persons have made false accusations to ruin my good name, and despoil me by harassing lawsuits of the savings of years of honest industry. I count among my acquaintances editor Andrew J King, former mayor John G Nichols, and the officers of the U S Internal Revenue Service.

ANNOTATION: *Los Angeles Star*, March 15th 1871.

REVEREND CRENSHAW: Mr. Lee, were you a native of our great city, you would know, as do we all, that the Celestial's letter was in fact written by the aforementioned Andrew Jackson King.

ANNOTATION: "Celestial" was a term applied to the Chinese as citizens of The Celestial Empire. Other appellations included "chinks," "semi-human Asiatics," "coolies," supposedly derived from the Chinese characters "ku" and "li" meaning "rented muscles," and John Chinaman, as in the popular mining tune from 1855:

CHORUS: I thought you'd open wide your ports
And let our merchants in
To barter for your crapes and teas
Their wares of wood and tin

I thought you'd cut your queue off, John
And don a Yankee coat
A collar high you'd raise, John
Around your dusky throat

Imagine that the truth, John,
You'd speak while under oath
But I find you'll lie and steal, too
Yes, John, you're up to both

LEE: Forgive me, Reverend, but it seems your story dispenses entirely with the Chinese view of these events.

REVEREND CRENSHAW: I am an eyewitness, sir.

LEE: In the courtroom?

REVEREND CRENSHAW: No, but almost immediately following.

(GEORGE FALL, *28, a Los Angeles City Councilman, appears.*)

GEORGE: Curly! Curly Crenshaw! Young sir!

(REVEREND CRENSHAW *goes to* GEORGE, *instantly changing into* CURLY CRENSHAW, *20, his younger self. His manner is now looser, sloppier, and physically more assured than* REVEREND CRENSHAW's. *Lights out on* LEE.)

GEORGE: You were inquiring at the Blue Wing about an anatomical anomaly.

CURLY: Pardon?

GEORGE: Chinese coochie.

CURLY: Yeah?

GEORGE: The slant, boy, the unique angle required for penetration—

(CURLY *and* GEORGE *fall silent as two nuns,* SISTER RASINDA, *30, and* SISTER PRUDENCIA *pass by.* CURLY *gives them the eye and they hurry on.*)

CURLY: I don't want no five-second peep for two bits at some green mansion in Nigger Alley—

GEORGE: No, I'm speaking of a unique opportunity. Fresh puss, previously under lock and key at Chinaman Sam's, now under new management, so to speak, of the Hong Chow Company. They kidnapped her and married her off to some Mongolian patsy as a way of taking legal ownership—I'll be damned, there he is!

(LEE TONG *appears, and* GEORGE *and* CURLY *immediately block his way.*)

CURLY: Howdy, John.

LEE TONG: No— (*Gesturing to self*) Tong. Tong.

GEORGE: Listen, Tongue, we understand congratulations are in order.

CURLY: Congratulations!   GEORGE: New little Chinese princess! Prettiest in town, so I hear.

LEE TONG: Sorry—?

GEORGE: Your wife, Tongue!

CURLY: Wife! Wife!

(CURLY *and* GEORGE *crowd* LEE TONG.)

GEORGE: Uncommon beautiful by all rumor. You got a popular girl! We're just wondering about your plans to share the wealth.

LEE TONG: Wealth?

GEORGE: You know the word wealth, John. Rich, like your fancy doctor brother.

LEE TONG: Girl? Share?   CURLY: Not many pretty girls in town.

GEORGE: That's right, Curly, hardly what you'd call a plethora of pulchritude in Los Angeles. Only three quarters of a woman to every man. Now what can you do with three quarters of a woman?

CURLY: I could manage.

GEORGE: Not many Chinese women in town either, are there, John?

LEE TONG: Tong, Tong!   CURLY: Not clean ones, anyways.

GEORGE: What do all those Chinamen do at night? Can't just pass one woman around like a whisky jug. How do you manage, Tongue?

(YO HING *appears. Seeing him,* GEORGE *and* CURLY *smirk and disappear.* SISTER RASINDA *returns, possibly looking for* CURLY.)

ANNOTATION: George Fall was a City Councilman, and his statistics are, in fact, correct. In 1871, only a handful of unmarried white women lived in Los Angeles, most of them Sisters of Charity or the Immaculate Heart of Mary.

(Lights out on YO HING *and* SISTER RASINDA *and up on* LEE *and* REVEREND CRENSHAW *in 1891.)*

LEE: Reverend Crenshaw, this seems a highly biased eye-witness account.

REVEREND CRENSHAW: Gospel truth. Although tis twenty years since, so memory may not serve precisely.

LEE: Memory tends to serve precisely what we wish to remember.

REVEREND CRENSHAW: Mister Lee, are you in a position of greater recall than I?

LEE: I've heard accounts that contradict your assertions.

REVEREND CRENSHAW: From John Chinaman himself?

LEE: I feel, in situations such as this, with memory colored by calamity or purged by passion, it's worthwhile to begin by acknowledging the basic humanity of all persons involved.

REVEREND CRENSHAW: The humanity of the Asiatics? Dear God—forgive me for taking the Lord's name in vain—but Goddammit, sir!

(Lights out on LEE.)

REVEREND CRENSHAW: Since the Mongolian violence in 1871, our city, our state, our country have succumbed to the Chinese curse! Have you any notion of how many Asiatics pollute Los Angeles with their presence this very moment?

ANNOTATION: There is no way to answer Reverend Crenshaw's alarmist demand as most of the 1890 census was destroyed in 1921 during a fire in the basement of the Commerce Building in Washington, DC.

REVEREND CRENSHAW: But enlighten me, sir, to use the Buddhist lingo, enlighten me about the relevant events from John's perspective! I am *eager*!

(*Lights out on* REVEREND CRENSHAW *and up on* YUT HO *and* LEE TONG *in a tiny bedroom with a tiny bed. Although he is dressed for sleep, she is still in her bridal outfit, and they are physically as far apart as possible in the cramped space.*)

LEE TONG: I know this wasn't your choice. (*No response*) It wasn't my idea, either. (*No response*) But I've just come to Gum Saan and I have nothing. You have nothing, too. Together we have each other. That's something, at least, isn't it?

(LEE TONG *tries to touch* YUT HO *in a tentative but intimate way. She remains impassive.*)

ANNOTATION: Rather than have all the Chinese characters sound like Hop Sing from *Bonanza*, when they are alone together the Cantonese they are speaking is rendered in English. This convention will be extended to all languages throughout the play.

LEE TONG: And here in Gold Mountain we're free!

YUT HO: Free?

LEE TONG: We don't have to do everything our parents tell us like in China.

(LEE TONG *tries to touch* YUT HO *again, with a bit more urgency, but there is still no response.*)

YUT HO: I was slave to my husband.

(LEE TONG *pulls away from* YUT HO.)

LEE TONG: I'm not that kind of husband.

YUT HO: We're both slave to Yo Hing.

LEE TONG: He is giving me money. A chance for life in Gold Mountain. He will not touch you. *(No response)* And neither will I. Unless you wish it. *(No response)* I'll never hurt you. I promise. That's not why I married you.

YUT HO: Then why?

LEE TONG: You are cold to me. But I see kindness in your coldness. I see inside, where you are even more beautiful. My brother—

YUT HO: Ah!

LEE TONG: You know my brother?

YUT HO: Chee Long Tong. The doctor.

LEE TONG: I'm a doctor, too! *(No response.)* Well, his apprentice. He's been in Gold Mountain for fifteen years—he came here as a boy—and he's very successful—

(GENE TONG, *26, a physician and* LEE TONG's *brother, appears isolated in light.*)

GENE: Because of Tong Yu.

LEE TONG: *(Going to* GENE*)* Your wife made you the envy of all Chinese?

GENE: White men, too. We're strangers in Gold Mountain, so we work harder than anyone else. Tong Yu keeps our accounts, works longer sometimes than I do.

LEE TONG: She has the tongue of a crow.

GENE: She must hide her tenderness in this lawless place, but I know her heart. She is the perfect wife—

LEE TONG: Perfect?!

GENE: Perfect for me. Don't be distracted by beauty, little brother, or even a soft polite voice.

LEE TONG: I'll choose well, Chee—you'll be proud.

GENE: Wait until you see what you need in a woman's heart. Then you will know she's perfect, too.

LEE TONG: Our parents don't choose! What a country!

(Lights out on GENE *as* LEE TONG *returns to* YUT HO.*)*

LEE TONG: Chee is highly intelligent. He's a doctor. He reads hearts.

YUT HO: You admire him.

LEE TONG: I must honor my older brother. He studied very hard and speaks beautiful English. Spanish, too!

YUT HO: *(Laughing)* I cannot help you *be* your brother!

LEE TONG: That's not what I want.

YUT HO: You want his respect.

LEE TONG: You read hearts, too. And you desire respect.

YUT HO: More than anything. But it's impossible.

LEE TONG: Did your first husband hurt you? Did Sam Yuen?

YUT HO: I saw Sam today. After our...ceremony.

(Lighting change as YUT HO *stands and becomes part of another scene with* SAM YUEN.*)*

SAM: He doesn't even speak English, does he?

YUT HO: He's studying hard.

SAM: Such a foolish choice. You're not marrying that boy, you're marrying Yo Hing.

YUT HO: I am protected by American law, by gold and diamond!

(YUT HO *shows* SAM *the ring, he reaches for it, and she pulls back.*)

SAM: Another foolish choice. That ring's too valuable to keep on your finger...if it's genuine. And if you run away with it, that's Yo Hing's clever excuse for your legal capture. Give it to me for safekeeping.

YUT HO: It makes me an American bride.

SAM: Now you'll be everyone's bride. The Hong Chow Company has plans for you. You think *I* worked you hard?

ANNOTATION: The rival company's opinion of the Hong Chow Company is a matter of public record:

SAM: Hong Chow isn't one of the old established Chinese companies, but a new concern gotten up here in Los Angeles for the purpose of trading upon the fears and necessities of friendless Chinamen, and of levying blackmail upon all.

ANNOTATION: *Los Angeles Star*, March 8-9, 1871.

LEE TONG: Of course he'd say that! They're competitors. He's cutthroat. Yo Hing promised we'd be left alone.

SAM: There is no marriage in this country, the land is infested with demons, and the people are given over to general wickedness. You don't want to stay here.

YUT HO: In China my family went hungry for days. My mother gleaned rice in the fields and sat on a handful to hide it until the workmen went home. Why would I want to go back?

LEE TONG: I don't want to go back either. The future is here!	SAM: Then stay. But with Nin Yung. You know I can protect you.

YUT HO: *(To* LEE TONG*)* When my father hanged himself, my mother sold me to pay for the coffin and I was shipped to San Francisco where I lived in a cage. Then here in Los Angeles for the Nin Yung Company I served only the most exclusive clientele. They say I'm beautiful. They say I'm worth—

SAM & YUT HO: Two thousand five hundred American dollars.

YUT HO: I've tried to escape three times.

SAM: You stole my watch! *(He advances menacingly.)*

YUT HO: But American deputies always find me. The company tied my sister to a tree and burned her to death in San Bernardino. A warning, they said.

SAM: We'll get you back, Yut Ho. You'll want to come back.

(Lights out on SAM.*)*

YUT HO: I cannot love you, Lee Tong. I am poison. My body is full of poison. I cannot love anyone.

LEE TONG: *(Going to her)* That's not what I'm asking—

YUT HO: *(Flinching, stopping him)* I cannot *touch* anyone. I have been touched too much.

LEE TONG: Do you miss China?

YUT HO: I can't tell.

LEE TONG: I'm happy to be here, but sometimes I miss it. There is an American word—

YUT HO: Homesickness.

LEE TONG: My brother gave me a cure! *(He gets a pinch of powder from a bag and mixes it in a cup of water.)*

YUT HO: There's no cure for what I have.

LEE TONG: It works for me.

YUT HO: What is it?

LEE TONG: *(Offering it to her)* China!

YUT HO: China in a cup?

LEE TONG: Chinese soil, just a pinch. Drink it in water and it's as good as going home.

(After a moment's hesitation, YUT HO smiles and drinks.)

YUT HO: I have something for you.

(YUT HO takes off the ring and gives it to LEE TONG.)

LEE TONG: But—

YUT HO: It's not safe for me to keep. That's a diamond.

LEE TONG: *(Examining it)* Really?

YUT HO: It's a test. Protect it and I'll believe you can protect me. You may read my heart.

(Lights out instantly on YUT HO and up on YO HING, who proffers a gun.)

YO: You'll need this.

LEE TONG: *(Quickly pocketing the ring)* I don't know how to use it.

YO: Learn. I got you a beautiful wife, now you have to defend her for me. Unless you'd like to do her job for her.

LEE TONG: She's done working!

YO: *(Grabbing LEE TONG roughly, sexual)* You know what happens to women who defy Sam Yuen. What happens to men who defy *me*?

(Lights out on LEE TONG.)

ANNOTATION: Yo Hing, by the way, was well known among the non-Chinese of Los Angeles, and was described by civic leaders as:

TRAFFORD: *(Appearing)* A fine fellow, suave, polished. Liked and respected by all decent citizens.

GEORGE: *(Appearing)* A man who in every way sustained the national reputation of his race for ways that are dark.

ANNOTATION: Several years later Yo Hing was dispatched by a rival, Wong Chew Shut, by two blows to the head with a Chinese cleaver.

(Lights out on everyone and up on LEE *and* REVEREND CRENSHAW.*)*

REVEREND CRENSHAW: I find your account remarkably detailed, sir, almost sell—sell— *(Having trouble remembering)*

LEE: Celestial?

REVEREND CRENSHAW: Exactly so! What is your real interest in the digit under discussion?

LEE: I'm a bone collector.

ANNOTATION: Between 1858 and 1876 bone collectors were hired by the Chueng Hau Association to exhume bodies of Chinese who died in the United States for return to their ancestral villages in China so their bones would receive the proper respect and offerings due the dead.

REVEREND CRENSHAW: This artifact is far too valuable to simply bury.

LEE: To you it is an artifact, a specimen for private delectation or scientific and cultural analysis. To my clients it is a human being still inhabited by a soul you hold hostage. I offer ransom. But I remain unconvinced of its authenticity.

REVEREND CRENSHAW: May I then enlighten you as to the events of October 24, 1871?

LEE: That is my earnest desire, Reverend sir.

REVEREND CRENSHAW: Everyone read of the marriage in the newspaper four days earlier—

ACT ONE 25

(Lights out on LEE *and* REVEREND CRENSHAW.*)*

ANNOTATION: Melican Marriage Ceremony: The White's marriage ceremony is becoming quite fashionable among the followers of Confucius in this city. Such a contract was consummated between a "John" and a "Maly" last evening by Justice Trafford. *Los Angeles Daily News,* October 21, 1871.

ANNOTATION OF THE ANNOTATION: Yut Ho was, in fact, married on March 3, 1871. The wedding performed on October 20 was for Ah Kit and Sung Kum. But following in the footsteps of historian Paul De Falla who wrote the widely known 1960 article *Lantern in the Western Sky,* this play conflates the two marriages, telescoping events to heighten tension and conflict.

(Lights up on SAM YUEN *in the dry goods store owned by* HILLIARD LOEWENSTEIN, *43, Prussian.)*

SAM: Me buy pistol.

HILLIARD: *(German accent)* What kind, Sam?

SAM: Shoot kind!

HILLIARD: Ah, but there is so much choice today! For instance, this Remington Rider is a classically-shaped derringer with a five-shot tubular magazine under the barrel and a single repeating action.

SAM: Very good.

*(*SAM *examines the gun. Lights up on* BIDDY MASON, *54, a midwife from Georgia and a former slave, and* ANN CAROL, *24, an Irish house servant.)*

BIDDY: *(Whispering)* It's called ergot.

ANN: *(Irish accent. Whispering)* Ergot? Is it dangerous?

BIDDY: I never lost a patient. But I don't overdose, neither. Too much and you get Saint Anthony's fire in all your limbs.

ANN: Does it always work?

BIDDY: Not always right off. If not, come back.

ANN: I need it to work. In a few weeks my employer will be able to tell and then I'm out the door. Presbyterians!

BIDDY: *(Measuring out some powder)* I'll measure out proper. I'm as good a Christian as them white folks and I'll ask Jesus to protect you.

HILLIARD: Here I've got a Smith & Wesson American No. 3, introduced just last year. They say it's a favorite of Jesse James.

ANN: They say the Chinese doctor has a new cure.

BIDDY: You gonna trust that foreigner Gene Tong with your precious body, child? Them Chinese been taking too much trade from born Americans. I sacrificed for what I got.

ANNOTATION: Biddy Mason came to Los Angeles in 1851 as a slave, but legally manumitted herself when she learned that California wasn't a slave state. A renowned midwife, she soon earned enough money to buy commercial property and in 1872 helped found the Los Angeles branch of the First African Methodist Episcopal Church.

*(*BIDDY *hands* ANN *the bag of powder and lights go out on them.)*

HILLIARD: Then I have this Colt 1862 Police, a .36 caliber lighter version of the 1860 Army.

*(*SAM *compares all the guns laid out side by side. Lights up on* EMIL *with* LYDIA SCHUBERT, *18, a Prussian girl.)*

EMIL: We're looking for a new soprano.

LYDIA: *(German accent)* Ach, I'm an alto.

EMIL: Even better! You know what an alto is, don't you?

LYDIA: What?

EMIL: A soprano who reads music.

ANNOTATION: Patrolman Emil Harris, co-founder of the Turn Verein Germania in 1871, later became the first Jewish police chief of Los Angeles, elected 1878.

LYDIA: Officer Harris, I don't need to join a group to sing. I sing on my own.

HILLIARD: Or there's this Remington Model 1863 Army and Roger & Spencer Army Revolver, both U S Army handguns.

EMIL: It's not just singing— the men learn gymnastics, and we study German history—

HILLIARD: Made when the Army's demands exceeded Colt's capacity and they had to turn to other sources.

(Lights out on HILLIARD *and* SAM *and up on* ESTEBAN SANCHEZ, *30, a uniformed policeman from Mexico having a drink at the Blue Wing Saloon with tavern-owner* ROBERT THOMPSON, *41.)*

THOMPSON: To rule the world is dogma, a creed, a holy tradition of China, and now are combined the circumstances that promise realization of this national dream—a tradition hoary with the frosts of centuries.

LYDIA: The history of Germany! How much history can there be for a country less than a year old? I'm Prussian, not German, no, not even Prussian, Officer Harris, American! I live here, now, and there is a reason my father brought me.

(SANCHEZ raises his glass in agreement, then downs his whisky. THOMPSON offers more.)

ANNOTATION: This quote is actually from *The Last Days of the Republic*, written by P W Donner in 1880, but it so accurately depicts the sentiments of many in the western states that it is reproduced here. Robert Thompson, saloon keeper, never lived to read it, of course, as you shall see.

SANCHEZ: *No mas, senor.* I am on duty.

EMIL: You should be proud to be German. I'm proud that I helped establish the Turn Verein Germania in Los Angeles during a few precious moments I could steal away from my duties hypothecating the obstreperous citizenry of our metropolis.

LYDIA: You are married, Herr Harris. It is not proper I am speaking with you.

(With a flirtatious flounce, LYDIA turns to go. EMIL follows as the lights go out on them.)

SANCHEZ: I knew Joaquin Murrietta.

THOMPSON: Did you now?

ANNOTATION: Joaquin Murrietta was a Californio bandit famous for eluding American authorities. When he was finally killed, his pickled head toured the state.

SANCHEZ: Murrietta had no love of the Chinaman. But he did say he loved the smell of his blood. And told how he tied six miners from the flowery kingdom together by their— *(He gestures.)* —Hair—

THOMPSON: Their queues—

SANCHEZ: —And slowly slit their throats.

(Lights out on THOMPSON and SANCHEZ and up on HILLIARD speaking to YO HING who stands exactly as SAM did, examining guns. CURLY stands nearby, admiring the

*guns. In a different area [*GENE TONG's *herbalist office],* LEE
TONG *is preparing an herbal remedy.)*

HILLIARD: Here, Mister Hing, is a fine Starr Double-
Action Model, a solid-frame revolver, unlike the open-
frame Colts.

YO: Me like.

(BIDDY *comes into the* LOEWENSTEINS' *store.* ROSA *goes to
help her.)*

HILLIARD: *(Demonstrating)* This is a double-action
revolver—

HILLIARD: Where it's not necessary—	ROSA: Good afternoon, Mrs Mason.
HILLIARD: —To cock the hammer before firing—	BIDDY: Good afternoon, Mrs Loewenstein. Just looking.

HILLIARD: —The trigger pull brings it back then
releases it—

YO: Me take.

(YO HING *takes the gun and enters the herbalist office,
becoming* GENE TONG.)

ROSA: Mrs Mason, is your son-in-law feeling better?

BIDDY: Yes, indeed, Mrs Loewenstein, Charles is doing
just fine. Thank you for asking.

LEE TONG: Chee?

GENE: Lee?

LEE TONG: Did I do wrong?

(Lights out on BIDDY, CURLY, HILLIARD, ROSA, *and* YO.)

GENE: Isn't it obvious you're being used? Did Yo Hing
pay you to marry this girl?

LEE TONG: Yes.

GENE: How much?

LEE TONG: More than you could give me, more than I could earn in years.

GENE: Do you know what it means to take a wife? How you are responsible—?

LEE TONG: I see you and Tong Yu—

GENE: Do you truly respect her? Or just feel sorry for her?

(LEE TONG *is silent.*)

GENE: Here.

(GENE *passes some herbs to* LEE TONG, *who carefully crushes them. They continue to work together with clocklike precision.*)

GENE: Does being married make you feel American?

LEE TONG: You're American. You speak their language.

GENE: You cannot buy respect with a wife. Our business prospers because I welcome Americans to our store, treat them well, make myself part of their community, deliberately, slowly. But I am not foolish enough to think myself one of them.

LEE TONG: You have their education, their religion.

GENE: My Christian education didn't make me Christian.

LEE TONG: I'll become a Christian and leave Chinese superstition behind.

GENE: Lee, you've been in Gold Mountain one month. You've no idea of American superstition, especially about us. I promised our mother I'd take care of you—

LEE TONG: And you do—

(TONG YU, 25, GENE's *wife, brings in some containers.*)

GENE: Tong Yu, congratulate my brother. He's just been married in a romantic American legal proceeding.

TONG YU: That fast? Barbaric! To whom?

LEE TONG: Yut Ho.

TONG YU: She's a bad girl.

LEE TONG: She's my wife!

TONG YU: It's not her fault, but she's a bad girl.

LEE TONG: Chee, your wife is disrespectful.

GENE: You would do well to listen to her. Tong Yu is always right.

TONG YU: Unfortunately.

(LEE TONG works silently.)

TONG YU: Whatever has happened to her, you must honor her now. Be kind to her. Her life has been hard.

LEE TONG: How do you know?

(GENE and TONG YU exchange a glance. LEE TONG sees and looks down.)

GENE: My brother even has some money to start his new family.

TONG YU: From?

LEE TONG: Yo Hing.

(TONG YU just looks disapproving.)

LEE TONG: I know he's Hakka—

TONG YU: Hakka, Punti, makes no difference to me. But Hong Chow is a bad company, and Yo Hing's an evil man. Last year his men were arrested for tying some poor woman to a stake, whipping and beating her. Now he's out for revenge on everyone who informed on them.

GENE: My brother is also converting to Christianity.

(TONG YU spits.)

LEE TONG: It's the American thing to do.

(They don't respond.)

LEE TONG: You talk about America all the time! You talked me into coming here. Escape the restrictions of China! Become a new man in Los Angeles like you did, where no one reminds you of tradition, your place—

TONG YU: Become a new man, a respected man like your brother, but not a fool.

LEE TONG: Where people come from all over the world—

TONG YU: With strange ideas—

LEE TONG: New ideas! Freedom! Clean paper, fresh ink to write with!

TONG YU: In all different languages—nobody understands anybody—in China everyone understands—

LEE TONG: Here you can have any religion you want.

(They don't respond.)

LEE TONG: It's what you say.

GENE: You are truly converting?

LEE TONG: Perhaps.

GENE: Then you must learn to turn the other cheek.

LEE TONG: What's that?

GENE: It's Christian. When someone does this— *(Slaps* LEE TONG, *hard)* —You turn your other cheek so they can do it again.

(GENE starts to slap LEE TONG again, but LEE TONG grabs his hand. A bit of blood drips from LEE TONG's lip.)

GENE: Now *that's* what an American would do. *Not* what a Christian would do.

(Lights up on REVEREND CRENSHAW as GENE, LEE TONG and TONG YU freeze.)

REVEREND CRENSHAW: Whose history is this, Mister Lee? Whose finger? As a Christian I am reminded of the days our Roman persecution. The calumny!

(In full view, LEE TONG changes costume elements to become LEE. Lights go out on GENE and TONG YU.)

LEE: I'm only endeavoring to understand all elements of a diabolically contradictory narrative.

REVEREND CRENSHAW: Diabolic indeed! I am grateful, at least, that you acknowledge the capability—no—guilt—

LEE: Culpability?

REVEREND CRENSHAW: Culpability! Of the yellow devils themselves. Their tong war endangering the whole city! Have you no sense of justice, sir?

LEE: *(After a moment)* Reverend Crenshaw, can you see my face?

REVEREND CRENSHAW: Beg pardon?

LEE: I cut myself shaving earlier today and suspect there may be blood on my face. Do you see any?

REVEREND CRENSHAW: *(Peers)* No, sir. Your face is fine.

LEE: *(Wiping the blood)* Much obliged, Reverend. And apologies for my poor attempts to amend your tale. Justice requires accuracy, so we must have all the facts. Please proceed. From your personal standpoint, of course.

REVEREND CRENSHAW: My own personal standpoint at approximately four in the afternoon on that terrible day was in Robert Thompson's Blue Wing Saloon—

(THOMPSON *appears.*)

REVEREND CRENSHAW: Where I was known—back then—

(REVEREND CRENSHAW *becomes* CURLY.)

CURLY: —To occasionally renew my acquaintance with John Barleycorn. But so did everyone else, including Officer Jesus Bilderrain—

(BILDERRAIN, *32, a uniformed policeman from Mexico, appears with a glass.* THOMPSON *is pouring him a drink.*)

BILDERRAIN: Just a small one. I'm on duty.

REVEREND CRENSHAW: And Sheriff James Burns.

(JAMES BURNS, *39, appears and accepts a drink from* THOMPSON *as* CURLY *joins him.*)

BURNS: *(Brooklyn accent)* Curly, you rascal, I can't make you a deputy!

CURLY: I can do as good as anybody you got now.

BURNS: That ain't the point—it's budget. It's always budget, no matter what, the reason for no is always budget.

CURLY: I wanna kick some ass. Get me a little respect!

BURNS: In the Sheriff's Department of Los Angeles County we keep order. We do not kick ass. Officially.

(BURNS *clinks glasses with* BILDERRAIN.)

BURNS: How is your beautiful wife, Mister Thompson?

| THOMPSON: Due to give me my first child any day now! | CURLY: Keep order? Half the bandits get away, the other half bribe the judge. It's not right! |

BURNS: Nostalgic for the Vigilance Committee? Taking the law into your own hands?

CURLY: At least justice was served.

BURNS: Those were the old days—we're American now. Real jury trials!

CURLY: You could get away with hiring me. Your term's almost up, ain't it? You can do whatever you want.

BURNS: Now you're advocating corruption, Curly— another form of lawlessness. The opposite of justice. We're growing this embryonic civitas right and proper—

CURLY: *(Overlapping)* Civitas?

BURNS: —So it matches the beauty of our gardens and country places where the perfumes of myriads of plants and flowers diffuse the air. *(Takes a deep breath)* Have you ever smelled sweeter?

CURLY: I smell horseshit.

BURNS: Also a fine, natural odor! Los Angeles is a modern Damascus, the Pearl of the Orient.

ANNOTATION: Sheriff Burns never said this, of course. His Edenic description of Los Angeles came from Reverend J W Hough writing in the *Los Angeles Star* on May 28th, 1873. He goes on:

BURNS: I discern a promise of a mighty inland traffic, which, unless diverted when the railroad systems of the region shall be determined, must make Los Angeles the second city in California. *(Saluting as he leaves)* Someday, young Curly, some day!

CURLY: And that's why you don't want a school teacher for Sheriff.

THOMPSON: *(Pouring more drinks for* BILDERRAIN *and* CURLY*)* And that's why they ran him outta office. His opponent bought a mess of votes with drinks on election day—I made out like a bandit!

ANNOTATION: According to the *Los Angeles Star*, on September 6th, 1871, with only twenty four hundred registered voters, there was drunk in the city of Los

Angeles during the state-wide primary election seven
thousand lagers, three thousand whiskeys, and two
thousand glasses of wine.

(They clink glasses and drink. Lights up on HILLIARD
LOEWENSTEIN *and* WONG TUCK, *25, a Chinese house
servant looking at the guns just as* SAM *and* YO *did.)*

HILLIARD: No, Wong, I can't. *(Starts putting guns away.)*

TUCK: Please, I beg!

HILLIARD: You'll just get in trouble.

*(*ROSA LOEWENSTEIN, *35,* HILLIARD's *wife, appears,
working in the store but eavesdropping as well.)*

TUCK: All Chinaman got guns!	CURLY: Lotta Chinamen buying guns today.
TUCK: I need, too!	

HILLIARD: Buying a gun's the first step toward getting
shot.

*(*ROSA *continues working as* HILLIARD *puts the guns away.*
TUCK *refuses to leave.)*

BILDERRAIN: Highbinders arming for a tong war?

CURLY: Wish I had a gun. They're after our cocks, you
know.

*(*BILDERRAIN *and* THOMPSON *look at* CURLY *then at each
other.)*

TUCK: Missus, I need—

ROSA: Hilliard—

HILLIARD: I said no, Rosa.

THOMPSON: How's that, Curly?

ROSA: We have a responsibility, dear, if something's happening—	CURLY: Theirs are so dinky, they want our—
TUCK: Big war!	CURLY: —Big ones.

ROSA: He works for us.

(HILLIARD *continues locking up the guns, ignoring* ROSA *and* TUCK. THOMPSON *leaves.*)

CURLY: It's tradition or something. They cut them off and keep 'em.

ANNOTATION: From the Guangdong region in China comes the legend of the beautiful Hu Li Jung, a genital thieving fox spirit traditionally thought to wander the countryside in search of male victims.

CURLY: —They put 'em in a kind of cock museum.

ROSA: He doesn't drink, he doesn't quarrel—

ROSA: He's not idle or prone to change, gives no eye service—	CURLY: I hear they're starting one right here in Nigger Alley.

(BILDERRAIN *bursts out laughing.*)

ROSA: He's patient, respectful— Extremely quick to learn—	CURLY: Looking for black cocks— Red cocks, but white cocks especially.

ROSA: Faithful to instructions, and makes no fuss.

(GEORGE FALL *joins the men in the saloon, looking smug.* HILLIARD *pointedly locks the guns up.*)

GEORGE: *(An announcement)* Gentlemen—

HILLIARD: No! *(Leaves)*

GEORGE: —I've secured the fire hose!

(BILDERRAIN *bursts out laughing again.*)

GEORGE: *(Hurt)* All the way from San Francisco! Just arrived today. No more bucket brigades!

BILDERRAIN: *(Giving* GEORGE *a drink)* Congratulations, George. On the house. I'm sure Thompson won't mind.

(Keeping an eye out for HILLIARD, ROSA *sneaks* TUCK *a hatchet. With a grateful nod, he tries to hide it in his clothes.)*

BILDERRAIN: Look out John Chinaman doesn't steal your hose!

*(*BILDERRAIN *and* CURLY *laugh.)*

GEORGE: They've practically taken over San Francisco! Ruining the economy. We've worked hard to create a civilization in this wilderness, and we can't let these barbarians take it away!

*(*EMIL *comes into the* LOEWENSTEINS' *store.* TUCK *almost bumps into him as he leaves quickly with the hatchet.)*

EMIL: Have you thought about the Turn Verein, Frau Loewenstein?

GEORGE: Every branch of industry in the State of California swarms with Chinese.

*(*HILLIARD *comes back in.* ROSARIO, 25, THOMPSON's *pregnant wife, comes in and starts cleaning the bar.)*

ROSA: *(To distract* HILLIARD, *who looks after the departing* TUCK*)* Hilliard, save me from this proselytizing madman!

EMIL: A confraternity celebrating united Germany! Not just songs and exercise—we do stage shows—it's uproarious.

GEORGE: Can we compete with a barbarous race, devoid of energy and careless of the State's weal?

HILLIARD: I've heard about your shows, Emil. You all dressed up as a schwartzer—blacking your face, disgraceful and undignified.

GEORGE: Sunk in their own debasement, having no voice in government, how long—would it be ere ruin would plunge the State into anarchy?

EMIL: It's harmless high spirits, Hilliard.

GEORGE: Working men must step to the front—

HILLIARD: Last month you even disguised yourself as Chinese!

GEORGE: —And hurl back the tide of barbarous invaders!

(BILDERRAIN *and* CURLY *cheer and raise their glasses with* GEORGE.)

EMIL: I had to give it up, however, as everyone was calling me Ching Ling Chinaman and chasing me!

(GEORGE *drains his glass and leaves. Lights up on* SAM *handing* AH CHOY *a gun)*

SAM: Yo Hing's in Beaudry Block.

HILLIARD: Don't know how you can show your face at temple after such an escapade.

AH CHOY: Where's that?

SAM: East end of the alley. Next to Doctor Tong's.

(*Lights up on* LEE TONG *nursing his cut lip.* BIDDY *comes in.* LEE TONG *regards* BIDDY *somewhat suspiciously as she checks out* GENE's *wares.* AH CHOY *starts to leave, then turns back to* SAM.)

AH CHOY: When the cobra is unable to release its venom fully, it vents its anger by biting wood and grass. Afterwards no one who touches the poisoned dead branches will escape death.

SAM: What? What?!

(AH CHOY *disappears. Lights out on* SAM)

BIDDY: Is Doctor Tong in?

LEE TONG: He no here. (*After a moment*) What you want?

BIDDY: Oh, I'll know it when I see it.

GENE: *(Coming in with medicine)* Mrs Mason—we're honored. This is my brother, Lee.

LEE TONG: Hello.

GENE: What can I help you with?

BIDDY: Nothing. Just looking. You have a fine store, Mister Tong. The envy of the neighborhood.

GENE: That's kind of you to say, Mrs Mason. *(Applying medicine to* LEE TONG's *lip.) Lay how-seung yao-mo see-ah?* [How's your lip?]

(THOMPSON *returns, and as he passes* ROSARIO *he caresses her pregnant belly and she affectionately slaps him. He kisses her hair, which she enjoys.)*

LEE TONG: *Ho dee-lah.* [Better.]

BILDERRAIN: Now that the railroad's done, John Chinaman's moving south.

(GENE *pats his brother affectionately.)*

GENE: *O woy-mm-gee, nguor doo mm-gee gee gay gom dai lic.* [Sorry. I didn't think I slapped you that hard.]

CURLY: New opium den or gambling hall in Nigger Alley every week, seems like.

(LEE TONG *grabs his brother's hand.)*

LEE TONG: *Sueong-la.* [It's all right.] *(Digs in his pocket) Lay hoy mm hoy-yee bong-nguor bow goo gee?* [Can you keep this safe for me?] *(Gives* GENE YUT HO's *ring) High Yut Ho bga guy-gee. Ho gwai jong gwai.* [It's Yut Ho's ring. Very valuable.]

GENE: *(Ostentatiously putting the ring on his pinky) Ngam-nguor dai woi! Nguor mm bay-fan-lay lah!* [It fits! I may not give it back!]

ROSARIO: *Por lo menos los estamos manteniendo fuera de Sonoratown.* [At least we're keeping them out of Sonoratown.]

BIDDY: Doctor Tong, have you any ergot?

LEE TONG: Ergot?

BILDERRAIN: *¡Ah! Usted está hablando del letrero, ¿Verdad?* [Oh, you mean that sign?]

GENE: A fungus, isn't it?

THOMPSON: *¿Que letrero?* [What sign?]

BIDDY: You don't carry it?

ROSARIO: *Un letrero que está puesto en Sonoratown* [A sign posted in Sonoratown.]

GENE: Chinese use something else.

BILDERRAIN: *Dice que ningún Chino pagano puede establecerse allí. Y todo Celestial ¡debe largarse!* [It said no heathen Chinese could settle there—]

BIDDY: For what?

GENE: For the same purpose as ergot. But it's better.

BILDERRAIN: *—Y todo los Celestiales deben huir.* [—and all the Celestials should run away.]

LEE TONG: *Lay gong-gan mut yeah-ah?* [What are you talking about?]

CURLY: What're you talking about?

GENE: *Ban mao* [Chinese blistering beetle.]

THOMPSON: Rosario saw a sign posted.

(GENE *pours some dead red and black beetles out for* BIDDY *to see.*)

GENE: You'd call it mylabris, or Chinese blistering beetle.

ROSARIO: *¡Vi dos!* [I saw two of them!]

BIDDY: Beetles! Sounds like a heathen cure.

THOMPSON: It warned the heathen Chinee to keep outta Sonoratown.

(YUT HO *comes into the store with some wrapped food. She and* BIDDY *catch each others' gaze and look quickly away.* YUT HO *hands the food to* LEE TONG, *they bow to each other respectfully and she hurries out of sight.*)

GENE: Works against cancers, tumors, growths, swellings—

BILDERRAIN & THOMPSON: And to cut their lucky!

(BILDERRAIN, CURLY *and* THOMPSON *laugh and clink glasses and the lights go out on them.* GENE *crushes some of the beetles to powder and scoops it into a tiny bag.*)

ANNOTATION: Sonoratown, just north of the central plaza and Calle de los Negros, was so named because it was first settled by Sonoran Mexicans.

LEE TONG: *Qing mm qing dough kuoy mong-gee Yut Ho goy-yeung? Ho-chee ho mm jean-jong kuoy gom. Lay deem-gai yew bong guor-ga hock-gwai? Kuoy tong-nguor day jan san-yee woi!* [Did you see the look she just gave Yut Ho? It wasn't very respectful, was it? What are you doing helping this black woman? She's our competitor, isn't she?]

(ROSARIO *picks up a chair.* THOMPSON *quickly takes it from her. She kisses him.*)

ANNOTATION: In 1933 when Chinatown was demolished to make way for Union Station, Chinese residents were moved to New Chinatown—on the site of Sonoratown.

GENE: *How lun kuoy-woi tong nguor-day mai four. Kuoy yao mm-high dai-foo, kuoy tse-but guor high jop-ma. Mm-woi tong nguor-day jang sang yee.* [If she decides she likes it, we'll be her supplier.

She's not a doctor, she's a
midwife—by no means
our competition.]

BIDDY: Puts a stop to growths and swellings of all
kinds you say?

(EUGENE MEYER, *30, a French dry goods merchant, comes
into* LOEWENSTEINS' *store.* ROSARIO *and* THOMPSON *step
away from the others and kiss some more.*)

GENE: As good as ergot. Or any Christian remedy.

EUGENE: *Bonjour, Hilliard.*   BIDDY: Then I'll be
Guten tag, Emil.   purchasing me a dose.

(*Everyone in* LOEWENSTEINS' *nods to* EUGENE. CURLY
spies on the canoodling THOMPSONS.)

HILLIARD: Emil, why don't you invite Eugene to join
your Turn Verein?

LEE TONG: You know my wife?

BIDDY: Who?

EUGENE: Those German minstrels?

LEE TONG: Yut Ho. My wife.

BIDDY: You married that   EMIL: Don't worry,
poor child?   Eugene, you'd never be
                                admitted.

LEE TONG: You know? Why you look— (*Makes a face*)

LEE TONG: —Bad face at   EUGENE: Why, don't you
her?   take Jews? Real Jews, I
                                mean.

GENE: *Lee, sao sang.* [Lee,   EMIL: I'm as Jewish as
shut up.]   you are.

BIDDY: I...helped her one time.

LEE TONG: What you mean?   EMIL: But we don't take
                                Frenchmen.

LEE TONG: *Bong kuoy, dee-meh-ah?* [What does she mean, she helped?]

BIDDY: She needed my help. That's all I will say.

(Lights out instantly on everyone and up simultaneously on YUT HO *cornered in her room by* AH CHOY, *gun in hand.)*

AH CHOY: Come with me back to the Nin Yung Company and you'll save Yo Hing's life.

YUT HO: Why should I save Yo Hing?

AH CHOY: And the life of your pretty young husband.

YUT HO: I'm not going back.

*(*AH CHOY *raises his gun to pistol whip* YUT HO.)*

YUT HO: I'm no good to anyone disfigured.

*(*AH CHOY *grabs* YUT HO.)*

YUT HO: *(Calling out)* Lee Tong!

(Lights out instantly on YUT HO *and* AH CHOY *and up on the group in the Blue Wing. They're all pretty drunk.)*

CURLY: Not gonna let them thievin' Chinee steal California!

ROSARIO: *¡Ustedes nos la robaron!* [You stole it from us!]

CURLY: What'd she say?

ROSARIO: *Ustedes, Gringos nos robaron California a los Mexicanos.* [You Gringos stole California from the Mexicans.]

BILDERRAIN: The gringos stole California from the Mexicans!

THOMPSON: Who stole it from the Spanish!

ROSARIO: *¡Quien se la robo a los indios!* [Who stole it from the Indians!]

BILDERRAIN: Who stole it from the Indians!

CURLY: We didn't steal California! We won it in a war, didn't we?

(Lights out instantly on the bar and up on GENE's *store.)*

LEE TONG: You say Yut Ho bad woman.

BIDDY: I said nothing of the kind.

LEE TONG: You say!   GENE: *Sao sang chun-choi,*
                                      kuoy hi nguor-day geh hoc-
                                      yan! [Shut up, you idiot!]

BIDDY: She can't help what   GENE: *Kuoy high ngor-day*
she is.   *geh hock-yan!* [She's our
                                      customer!]

LEE TONG: Black—demon—kill babies!

BIDDY: *(Starting to leave)* Excuse me, Doctor Tong.

LEE TONG: How you say? Nig-gah?

BIDDY: *(Stops, turns toward him slowly)* Poor little yellow
man, what you got? Nothing. 'Cept maybe a punk for
a wife, and that ain't much. What I got? Every baby
born here owe me its life. I got respect. I got freedom.
I got real estate. You got nothing. Not even a word of
English.

LEE TONG: *(Venomously)* Nig-gah.

BIDDY: Well. *One* word. But *I* ain't the one living in
Nigger Alley.

YUT HO: *(Off)* Lee Tong, *nguor geh nam-yan!* [Lee Tong!
My husband!]

LEE TONG: Yut Ho!

*(*LEE TONG *runs out. Lights out instantly on* GENE's *store
and up on the* LOEWENSTEINS' *store.)*

EUGENE: Without hesitation I joined your Hebrew
Benevolent Society, and with some reluctance I became
an Odd Fellow at your persistent urging, Herr Harris,
but I will not betray the country of my birth by joining
the Turn Verein Germania.

EMIL: Meyer, Meyer, Meyer! Doesn't sound very French to me.

EUGENE: I'm as French as I am Jewish—

EMIL: What admirable fealty to a nation so pathetic it can't even settle on a government! Can't win a war!

EUGENE: United Germany is a curse! France, at least, isn't known for its pogroms!

EMIL: Twelve fifty-one—the Pastoreaux attacked Jews and again in 1320—

| EUGENE: That was the Middle Ages—! | HILLIARD: Gentlemen, gentlemen—! |

EMIL: *(Singing)*
Deutschland, Deutschland über alles
Über alles in der Welt

(EUGENE tries to out-sing EMIL.)

EUGENE:	EMIL:
Allons enfants de la Patrie	*Wenn es stets zu Schutz*
Le jour de gloire est arrivé.	*und Trutze brüderlich*
Contre nous, de la tyrannie—!	*zusammenhält.*

(Lights out instantly on the store and up on the bar.)

CURLY: Save our cocks!

ROSARIO: *¡Está loco!* [He's crazy!]

(BILDERRAIN and THOMPSON laugh.)

| CURLY: Kill the Chinese gelders! | THOMPSON: *¡Nomas esta borracho!* [He's just drunk!] |

| BILDERRAIN: The elders? | ROSARIO: *¡Roberto, sacalo de aqui! Va causar problemas!* [Roberto, throw him out! He's going to cause trouble!] |

CURLY: The gelders! Don't let 'em make capons outta you!

THOMPSON: *¡El no esta loco, tiene razon! Nos quieren joder!* [He's not crazy, he's right! They're out to get us!]

(Lights up on the LOEWENSTEINS' *store.* HILLIARD *and* ROSA *are trying to pull* EMIL *and* EUGENE *apart.)*

HILLIARD: The war ended last May!

ROSA: Not in our store!

CURLY: Save our cocks!

EMIL: *Ich unterrichte Sie, Deutschland zu beleidigen!* [I'll teach you to insult Germany!]

BILDERRAIN & CURLY: Save our cocks!

EUGENE: *Votre chant est terrible—!* [Your singing is terrible—!]

BILDERRAIN & CURLY: Save our cocks!

HILLIARD: There's a reason we all came here!

(Lights up on BIDDY *and* GENE. *He bows to* BIDDY.*)*

BILDERRAIN & CURLY: Save our cocks!

EUGENE: *—Et vous a volé l'air d'Autriche!* [—and you stole the tune from Austria!]

GENE: Mrs Mason, I have lost face.

BILDERRAIN, CURLY & THOMPSON: Save our cocks!

EMIL: French Communist!

GENE: I apologize for my brother.

BILDERRAIN, CURLY & THOMPSON: Save our cocks!

EUGENE: Prussian anti-Semite!

BIDDY: *(Taking out a coin)* How much for them beetles?

GENE: Keep your money, Mrs Mason.

BILDERRAIN, CURLY & THOMPSON: Save our cocks!

(BIDDY *looks startled as* GENE *hands her a bag of powder.*)

BILDERRAIN, CURLY, ROSARIO & THOMPSON: Save our cocks!	EUGENE: *Comment pouvez-vous vous appeler un juif?* [How can you call yourself a Jew?]

GENE: Professional courtesy.

BILDERRAIN, CURLY, ROSARIO & THOMPSON: Save our cocks!	ROSA: We're all Americans now!

(*A shot rings out. Everyone freezes. Lights up on* LEE TONG *standing over a prostrate* AH CHOY. LEE TONG *holds a gun and looks dazed. Blood gushes from* AH CHOY'S *neck.* YUT HO *is frozen nearby with a strange look on her face: some combination of shock, relief and horror—or even triumph as she realizes her new husband is capable of defending her.*)

BILDERRAIN: That came from Nigger Alley.

(BILDERRAIN, EMIL, *and* THOMPSON *all draw guns.*)

CURLY: (*Quietly*) Save our cocks...

(BILDERRAIN *and* CURLY *leave.* THOMPSON *starts to go, but* ROSARIO *grabs him.*)

EMIL: There's been some trouble among the Chinese.

ROSARIO: *Roberto, no te vayas. Ellos se encargaran de eso.* [Roberto, don't go. They'll take care of it.]	EUGENE: Afraid to finish what you started?

(*Lights up on a ramshackle doorway as* BILDERRAIN *approaches carefully, gun drawn.* CURLY *follows.*)

THOMPSON: *Si hay problemas, es malo para el negocio.* [If there's trouble, it's bad for business.]	EMIL: Hilliard started it, if I'm not mistaken, with his sly remark.

(BILDERRAIN *cracks open the door, peers in, then disappears inside.* CURLY *hangs back at first.*)

ROSARIO: *Calle de los Negros es muy peligrosa!* [Calle de los Negros is very dangerous!]	EMIL: I've got no time to re-enact the Franco-Prussian war.

(CURLY *peers in the door.* EMIL *leaves* LOEWENSTEINS' *store.*)

THOMPSON: *Rosario, Es nuestro pueblo también.* [It's our town, too, Rosario.]

(*Several shots ring out from inside the doorway.* CURLY *leaps back from the door.* THOMPSON *runs out of the bar.*)

ROSARIO: (*Running to the door after him*) No, Roberto!

(BILDERRAIN *staggers out of the doorway, bleeding from the shoulder. He drops his gun, puts his police whistle in his mouth and blows. Instant lights out everywhere except:*)

ANNOTATION: After blowing his police whistle, Officer Bilderrain was not seen again that night.

(*Lights up on* LEE TONG *and* YUT HO. *He is so stunned by his act that he barely reacts when* YUT HO *takes the gun from his hand.*)

YUT HO: We have to hide!

LEE TONG: (*Indicating the wounded* AH CHOY) But what about—?

YUT HO: The police will come—!

LEE TONG: We can't leave him—he's bleeding, choking—

YUT HO: Sam Yuen will come! Yo Hing will come! Everyone will be after us now.

LEE TONG: I didn't turn the other cheek...

(YUT HO *practically drags* LEE TONG *away as lights go out on them and up on the doorway.* CURLY *grabs*

BILDERRAIN'S *abandoned gun as* THOMPSON *approaches, gun drawn.)*

CURLY: The Mongolians shot Bilderrain!

THOMPSON: Where is he?

CURLY: Went to the doctor, I think.

(Shots ring out from inside the doorway. CURLY *and* THOMPSON *return fire. The shots from within cease, and after a moment* CURLY *and* THOMPSON *stop firing as well.* THOMPSON *approaches the doorway.)*

CURLY: There were at least a dozen in there!

THOMPSON: I'll look out after that!

*(*THOMPSON *peers into the door, then sticks his arm inside and starts shooting. His shots are returned, and one hits him in the chest. He staggers back.)*

CURLY: *(As* THOMPSON *falls at his feet)* White man killed!

(Lights out instantly on CURLY *and* THOMPSON *and up on* FRANK BAKER, *42, city marshall.)*

BAKER: White man killed!

(Lights up on GENE TONG *and* TONG YU.)*

GENE TONG & TONG YU: *(Quietly)* White man killed.

(Lights up on James BURNS *and* CRISTOBAL AGUILAR, *57, the Californio Mayor of Los Angeles, as well as [in a separate area]* SAM *and* CHINESE MAN, *guns drawn.)*

BURNS: White man killed!

CHINESE MAN & SAM: *Back gwai say-juor ah!* [White man killed!]   EVERYONE: White man killed!

(Lights on ROSARIO *cradling the dead* THOMPSON *in her arms.)*

ROSARIO: Roberto!

(Lights up on GEORGE FALL.)*

GEORGE: The Celestials are killing whites wholesale in Nigger Alley!

(Lights out on everyone but BAKER *and* GEORGE.)

BAKER: Surround the Coronel Block! Any Chinese attempting to escape will be shot on sight!

*(*GEORGE *jumps up onto a barrel.)*

GEORGE: We knew it would come to this! We remember with what professions of peace and goodwill the Chinese offered the Burlingame Treaty, and yet—

*(*CURLY *joins* BAKER, *and they both shoot at the ramshackle doorway as* GEORGE *continues. Shots are returned from inside.)*

GEORGE: —Scarce were the signatures dry upon the paper before occurred the horrible massacre of foreigners at Tien-tsin, June twenty-first, eighteen hundred and seventy. The French Consul and foreign merchants, their wives, daughters, and children, the Catholic priests and the Sisters of Mercy and about one hundred orphan children were cruelly murdered.	ANNOTATION: While witnesses later testified that George Fall exhorted the crowd, whipping it into a frenzied mob, this *particular* speech is based on an address made to the Social Science Association of America at Saratoga, New York on September 7th, 1877 by the Honorable Edwin R Meade, a former U S Congressman.

*(*ADOLPHO CELIS, *20, appears supporting* ROSARIO.)

GEORGE: These children had been gathered by the Sisters from the byways of the town—	CELIS: Don't let 'em get away! They're murderers!

GEORGE: —Where they had been left to die by their parents. The coolies set fire to the buildings occupied by the Sisters—

(ALEXANDER JOHNSON, *36, joins* BAKER *and* CURLY *as they shoot at the doorway. Shots are no longer returned.*)

| GEORGE: —Whom they dragged out into the streets. There they were stripped naked, outraged, exposed to the public gaze— | ALEXANDER: *(Irish accent)* Come on out, ye cowards! |

(LOUIS MENDEL, *35, joins* CELIS *and* ROSARIO.)

| GEORGE: —Their eyes plucked out, their breasts cut off— | CELIS: *Rosario, dejeme llevarla a su casa.* [Rosario, let me take you home.] |

(ROSARIO *pushes* CELIS *away.*)

| GEORGE: —Then ripped open, tore out their hearts— | CELIS: This innocent woman's lost her husband! |

(ROSARIO *runs off, with* CELIS *after her.*)

| MENDEL: *Töten Sie die Chinesen!* [Kill the Chinese!] | GEORGE: —And deliberately cut them in pieces, and divided them among the infuriated mob! |

| MENDEL: *Sie nehmen Arbeit von den annehmbaren Völkern!* [They're taking jobs away from decent folk!] | ALEXANDER: Looks like we got 'em. |

(*Everyone stops shooting.* CRISTOBAL AGUILAR *joins the men.*)

GEORGE: Capable of such deeds, can the injection of such a race into our body politic be viewed without anxiety and alarm?

(Silence for a moment)

AGUILAR: *(Spanish accent)* Looks like you've got it well in hand, Marshall. *(He leaves.)*

ANNOTATION: Mayor Cristobal Aguilar was not seen again that night.

(WONG TUCK runs out of the doorway with his hatchet, trying to escape.)

BAKER: There one goes!   ANN: Get him!

(EMIL appears and tackles the fleeing TUCK.)

TUCK: *Gao-mang-ah!* [Help   EMIL: Give me that
me, someone!]   hatchet!

(Everyone crowds around, but BAKER holds them back.)

BAKER: Step aside, everyone. Let the law operate.

(EMIL hauls TUCK to his feet and takes the hatchet away.)

BAKER: Now, John, what's this all about?

TUCK: Please, sir!

EMIL: He's the Loewenstein's servant.

BAKER: What were you doing with that hatchet?

TUCK: Me no fraid, me good, no hurt any man.

EMIL: I believe he's harmless, sir.

BAKER: I agree.

CROWD: *(Variously)* No! Hang him! *¡Cuelgenlo!* [Hang him!]

EMIL: Shall I take him to jail, sir, for his own safety?

BAKER: Excellent notion. Proceed, officer.

(EMIL starts off with TUCK, and BAKER leaves.)

ANNOTATION: And that was the last seen of Marshall Baker, chief of police, for the next three hours.

GEORGE: How can you even touch him? They're disgustingly filthy.

GEORGE: Nothing can exceed the noisome odors which exhale from their proximity—

MENDEL: We should hang the dirty laundry!

(The CROWD *begins to converge on* EMIL *and* TUCK.*)*

EMIL: Back off!

GEORGE: —And that such is a national characteristic is borne out by all travelers in China, from Abbe Huc to the present day!

OTHERS: Yeah! Hang 'em! String 'em up! He shot Thompson! Justice! Justice! Don't let 'em get away with it! ¡Justicia!

(The CROWD *completely overwhelms* EMIL *and he and* TUCK *disappear among them.* ANN *appears with some clothesline.)*

EMIL: I'm taking him to jail!

MENDEL: *Hängen Sie ihn!* [Hang him!]

OTHERS: *(Overlapping)* ¡Cuelgenlo! [Hang him!] *Pendrezle!* [Hang him!] Tie him his last necktie! Take him to the corral on Temple!

TUCK: No hurt! Please! Me sorry!

ANN: You'll be needing this.

EMIL: *Hürensohnen!* [Sons of whores!]

OTHERS: To New High Street! Make him dance on a string! Hang him!

(The CROWD *drags* TUCK *away, leaving* EMIL *struggling in* CURLY's *grip, his arms pinned behind him.* ROSA LOEWENSTEIN *appears, horrorstruck.)*

EMIL: Let me go, you devil!

OTHERS: *(Overlapping)* To the corral! There's a stout crossbeam there! Hang 'em high! Break his chinky neck! Show 'em what we're made of! This is our city!

EMIL: *(Breaking free of* CURLY*)* You idiot! They're going to hang him!

CURLY: And I'm gonna pull the rope!

*(*CURLY *runs after the* CROWD. EMIL *starts to follow, but* ROSA *calls to him.)*

ROSA: Emil, what are they—? I gave him that hatchet—!

GEORGE: They keep their own filthy customs, refuse to adopt American ways!

EMIL: I'm sorry, Mrs Loewenstein, I couldn't stop them!

GEORGE: They work for almost nothing, stealing jobs from good Americans!

(The CROWD *proceeds to hang* WONG TUCK, *who struggles as long as he can but eventually succumbs. This may be stylized, or even off stage with stylized audience reaction. Perhaps all of this is done in utter silence as* GEORGE *continues.)*

GEORGE: Every Chinaman is the devil incarnate, their touch is pollution, and justice to our race demands that they should not be allowed to settle on our soil!

(A hush or even a group sigh as everyone stands back to view their handiwork. Is the CROWD *stunned by its own violence?* GEORGE *looks at the dead* TUCK *with satisfaction.)*

ANNOTATION: *(Overcome with emotion)* The lynching of Wong Tuck represents the emotional climax of the first act of the play. Therefore, in order to blunt the emotional impact and reinforce the alienation effect, the moment is interrupted with this otherwise pointless annotation.

GEORGE: That's one.

(The CROWD *turns to him.)*

GEORGE: But there's plenty more in Nigger Alley!

ANNOTATION: What happens next best remains unannotated.

(The CROWD *shrieks with delight and shoots at the ramshackle doorway of the Coronel Block, shouting as the lights fade.)*

CROWD: *(Variously, all at once)* Get 'em all! They got gold! They got women! No justice, no peace! Filthy animals! *(Continuing under song)* Clean 'em out! Tear down the gambling halls! *Pendrez-les! ¡Cuelgenlos! Hängen Sie sie!* [Hang them!] Burn the opium dens! Hang 'em all! Purge our city! Make Los Angeles clean again! No Celestials, only angels!

CHORUS: I thought of rats and puppies, John,
You'd eaten your last fill
But on such slimy pot-pies, John
I'm told you dinner still

Oh, John, I've been deceived in you
And all your thieving clan
For our gold is all you're after, John
To get it while you can

END OF ACT ONE

ACT TWO

(LEE *and* REVEREND CRENSHAW)

LEE: A tragedy or justice served?

REVEREND CRENSHAW: Justice, certainly!

LEE: Vigilante justice.

REVEREND CRENSHAW: Only the Chinese Exclusion Act
of 1882 was a more noble attempt to preserve our way
of life. But tragic for its ultimate lack of effect.

LEE: Reverend, are you blind?

REVEREND CRENSHAW: I am celebrated for my vision,
sir!

LEE: What color is my hair?

REVEREND CRENSHAW: I beg your pardon?

LEE: The room is reasonably illuminated. My hair is
abundant and in plain view. What color?

REVEREND CRENSHAW: Brown.

LEE: It is black.

REVEREND CRENSHAW: Dark brown.

LEE: Black. *En Espanol: negro.* I've tested you all
evening. How long have you been sightless?

REVEREND CRENSHAW: *(After a moment)* Not quite a
year.

LEE: God's judgment?

REVEREND CRENSHAW: *(Gesturing to the opulent room)* God has shown me only mercy and favor—look around you. I have earned the respect of Man and God.

LEE: You can't have mercy without justice first.

REVEREND CRENSHAW: It's late.

LEE: I remain unsatisfied as to the provenance.

REVEREND CRENSHAW: Perhaps tomorrow—

LEE: No, sir. A riot ensued, that is clear. And at least one murder. *(Holding up the pinky)* How came you by this?

REVEREND CRENSHAW: For whose funeral have you come, sir?

LEE: This is all that remains of a man, Reverend. What became of the rest of him?

REVEREND CRENSHAW: My other prospective purchasers have no need of such assurance.

LEE: I will double the price.

(REVEREND CRENSHAW holds out his hand. LEE drops four twenty-dollar gold pieces into REVEREND CRENSHAW's hand.)

REVEREND CRENSHAW: That's eighty.

LEE: You'll receive the final twenty upon my satisfaction.

REVEREND CRENSHAW: *(Smiles)* Fair enough. We share a sense of justice, sir.

LEE: Indeed we do. Pray continue your tale.

REVEREND CRENSHAW: It is not a tale. It is the truth, sir.

LEE: Your truth.

REVEREND CRENSHAW: God's truth.

(Lights begin to come up on the open doorway, the unseen CROWD in the shadows outside, an orange glow within.)

REVEREND CRENSHAW: First, there was a fire.

(A cheer from the unseen CROWD *as lights dim on* LEE *and* REVEREND CRENSHAW.)

VARIOUS: Burn 'em out! Cauterize! Hey, that could spread! Who threw that fireball?

CURLY: *(Appearing, isolated in light)* I did! What of it?

VARIOUS: That's Don Antonio's adobe! Don't burn down the whole town! We don't wanna be another Chicago! My God, Chicago! Are you crazy? *¡No queremos otro Chicago!*

ANNOTATION: The great Chicago fire less than two weeks earlier was still big news. The events in Los Angeles drove the fire from the front pages of the nation's papers.

GEORGE: *(Appearing with the firehose)* C'mon, boys! Our first test!

(As others join him holding the hose.)

GEORGE: Turn on the water! We'll flush 'em out! *(Nothing)* Turn it on!

MAN: *(Off)* It is on!

(A groan from the CROWD. ESTEBAN SANCHEZ *and* CHARLES AUSTIN, *30, a former constable,appear with pickaxes and guns.)*

AUSTIN: Your hose is limp, George!

(Laughter from the unseen CROWD. ESTEBAN *and* AUSTIN *tear at the roof of Coronel Block with the pickaxes.)*

AUSTIN: We'll smoke 'em out!

ESTEBAN: *¡Cortaremos a través de esta brea en poco tiempo!* [We'll cut through this brea in no time!]

EMIL: *(Grabbing* CURLY*)* You've caused no end of trouble tonight. Where'd you get that fireball?

GEORGE: Try it again!

CURLY: Get your hands off!

GEORGE: Are you trying?

MAN: *(Off)* It's turned all the way up, George!

GEORGE: Goddammit! I just bought this thing!

(Laughter. AUSTIN starts shooting through the hole they've created in the roof.)

ESTEBAN: Don't shoot, don't shoot! Only if they do!

(One or two CHINESE MEN run out the door.)

CHINESE MEN: *Mm-ho seh! Mm-high nguor-day!* [Don't shoot! It's not us!]

(The unseen CROWD responds by immediately shooting the CHINESE MEN dead. They fall down as the CROWD cheers.)

VARIOUS: *¡Dos mas!* [Two more!] That's just the beginning! Two more we don't have to worry about! Hang 'em! They're already dead! Hang 'em anyway! *¡Cuelgenlos!* [Hang them!] *Hängen Sie sie!* [Hang them!] *Pendrez-les!* [Hang them!]

EMIL: Get on in there and put that out!

CURLY: I ain't going in there!

(Lights out on the bodies. ESTEBAN and AUSTIN jump down into Coronel Block through the hole in the roof. Lighting change as they disappear.)

EMIL: *(Dragging CURLY into the doorway) Blöde Amerikanerkind!* [Stupid American child!]

VARIOUS: Burn it all down! There are more in there! Put it out!

(Sound of stomping as the fire light goes out and the lights dim on the doorway and come up on GENE, LEE TONG, YUT HO, and TONG YU making their way through a tunnel. GENE and LEE TONG carry lanterns.)

LEE TONG: No more shots.

TONG YU: That doesn't mean we're safe.

YUT HO: Where does this tunnel go?

GENE: Under Coronel Block and Beaudry Block.

ANNOTATION: The existence of tunnels under
Chinatown is documented only in secondary sources
and remains a subject of considerable debate today. So
the following line may simply be a lie:

TONG YU: Chin Woa Company and Nin Yung
Company tunneled under all these buildings a few
years ago.

GENE: Now we know why.

LEE TONG: Where does it let out?

*(Sound of many footsteps thundering on wooden floorboards
above them.)*

YUT HO: They're in the building.

*(Lights fade on the tunnel and come up on the interior of
GENE's store. It's a shambles, and the CROWD races through
with lanterns, whooping and destroying, grabbing and
running. They are gone as quickly as they came. There is one
dead CHINESE MAN on the floor. CURLY runs into the room
and shoots the dead man once or twice. EMIL and ESTEBAN
follow him into the room.)*

EMIL: You're under arrest.

CURLY: Can't arrest me for shooting a dead man.

*(CURLY flees, laughing. EMIL makes a half-hearted effort to
go after him but stops at the door.)*

ESTEBAN: No good, Emil. Too many bad ones.

EMIL: And not enough of us.

ESTEBAN: *(Looking around the room)* Oficina de medico.
[Doctor's office.]

EMIL: I wonder how many cures were here.

ESTEBAN: He must have some money.

EMIL: If he did, it's gone. Over at his place, Sam Yuen had six thousand dollars in gold.

ESTEBAN: That's gone, too.

EMIL: Maybe not. It's well hidden.

ESTEBAN: ¿Dónde está? [Where is it?]

EMIL: It's in Sam's store.

ESTEBAN: As officers of the law we are obligated to protect Mister Yuen's property.

(ESTEBAN *and* EMIL *look at each other as the lights fade on them and come up on* LEE TONG, GENE, YUT HO *and* TONG YU *in the tunnel.*)

LEE TONG: Is that the way out?

GENE: Around that turn and then up. You and Yut Ho go first.

LEE TONG: Where does it put us?

TONG YU: Sanchez Street, just off the Plaza.

EMIL: *(Off)* Stop. By order of the police.

YUT HO: *Bay-yang jook-dough-la!* [We're dead!]

TONG YU: *Jiao-ah!* [No, keep going!]

(EMIL *and* ESTEBAN *show up behind the group, carrying a lantern, their guns, and a small chest.* GENE *and* TONG YU *stand between the policemen and* LEE TONG *and* YUT HO, *hiding them.*)

GENE: Officer Harris, is that you?

EMIL: Doctor Tong?

GENE: Yes.

EMIL: Who else is there?

GENE: My wife.

TONG YU: Hello.

(Sound of running feet and a few gunshots on the floor above. YUT HO *and* GENE *hold both lamps and motion for* YUT HO *and* LEE TONG, *who reluctantly sneak off into the darkness.)*

ESTEBAN: That is all?

GENE: Just the two of us. What's happening, Officer?

EMIL: We need to take you to jail.

GENE: We've done nothing.

EMIL: Jail is so nothing may be done to you. We will escort you, but we'll need to tie your hands.

*(*EMIL *motions to* ESTEBAN, *who puts down the chest in order to tie their hands.)*

GENE: Why? We're not criminals.

EMIL: If we tie you to us, we can hold onto you.

GENE: What is that you're carrying, officer?

ESTEBAN: *Nada.*   EMIL: That's not your
                                     business, doctor.

GENE: Is there looting?

EMIL: Yes, I'm afraid so.

GENE: My office?

EMIL: The government will reimburse you. Now come along.

(They turn and march back the other way, GENE *and* TONG YU *ahead, their hands tied.)*

TONG YU: *Kuoy day seung doi nguor-day-deem-te?* [What are they going to do with us?]

GENE: *Nguor lom nguor day*   ESTEBAN: We can't just
huo-yee sun kuoy-day.   parade Sam Yuen's chest
Yee-guo nguor day high   around the Plaza. How
gam-yook-dough, huo   can we explain it?

lan-gay-gow on-chueng.
[I think we can trust these
two. If they put us in jail,
we may be safe.]

EMIL: I have an idea.

(Lights out on them and up on the doorway and the alley in front of it. Shouts, screams, gunshots, and various people dashing about. EMIL, ESTEBAN, GENE and YUT HO come through the doorway. No one sees them yet.)

EMIL: Can you take them to jail?

ESTEBAN: *Si.*

EMIL: *(Reaching for the chest)* I'll take care of this.

ESTEBAN: *(Not relinquishing the chest)* What are you doing with it?

EMIL: There's no time. I'll be back in a moment.

(ESTEBAN reluctantly parts with the chest, and EMIL disappears with it.)

GENE: Whose was that, Officer?

ESTEBAN: Ours. Now hurry before anyone sees us.

(Suddenly the unseen CROWD is heard around them.)

AUSTIN: Two more! *¡Agarenlos!* [Get them!]

AUSTIN: That's the rich doctor!	WOMAN IN CROWD: He works Chinese spells!

ESTEBAN: I'm taking them to jail. *(Brandishes his gun)* Stay back!

(SHERIFF JAMES BURNS suddenly appears atop the barrel GEORGE used earlier.)

BURNS: People of Los Angeles! Be reasonable! The Los Angeles County Sheriff's Department is in control. Go back to your homes, and we'll take care of any

evil-doers—! By the light of day you will see this is
madness, see what we've become—

AUSTIN: ¡*Los chinos asesinos*   WOMAN IN CROWD: You
se están saliendo con la suya!   can't take care of
[The Chinese get away with   anything!
murder!]

BURNS: Can't we all just get—?

(BURNS' *speech is interrupted when he falls through the lid
of the barrel, much to the vocal amusement of the* CROWD.
At the same moment someone shoots ESTEBAN'S *gun out of
his hand. The* CROWD *shrieks its approval and the pool of
light around* ESTEBAN, GENE *and* TONG YU *tightens as the
crowd moves closer.*)

ESTEBAN: Stay behind me!   TONG YU: *Mm ho bay kuoy
                                day dai-nguor-jiao!* [Don't
                                let them take me!]

GENE: *Tong Yu, jook sat   ALEXANDER: Quick, get
nguor!* [Tong Yu, hold onto   'em now!
me!]

AUSTIN: ¡*Agarenlos!* [Grab   WOMAN IN CROWD:
them!]   They'll get away!

(*The circle of light around* ESTEBAN, GENE *and* TONG YU
tightens and disappears as the CROWD *closes in.*)

VARIOUS: Hang 'em both! We can't hang a woman!
Give me the woman! Search their pockets! He's got a
ring! Where's the rope? Who's got the rope?

(*Lights up on* EMIL *with* LYDIA. *She's staring in
astonishment at the chest in her hands.*)

LYDIA: I can't!

EMIL: Just for a day or two. I'll come get it when things
die down.

LYDIA: I don't have any place to put it.

EMIL: I don't either, but we have to keep it safe for Sam.

LYDIA: You mean you're giving it back?

EMIL: I'm going to—

(*Sound of the* CROWD *shouting in the distance.*)

LYDIA: Why give it to me and not your wife?

EMIL: I've got to go! Thank you!

LYDIA: Emil! Emil! I don't want this!

(*Lights fade on* LYDIA *and come up on* HENRY HAZARD *escorting* SAM YUEN *and another* CHINESE MAN.)

HENRY: You'll be safe in the courthouse.

SAM: (*Proffering money*) Here, most honored sir.

HENRY: What's that?

SAM: For you, you take!

HENRY: I don't want your money! Put that away!

AUSTIN: (*Appearing*) I'll take them Mongolians off your hands.

HENRY: No thank you, sir, I'm managing.

AUSTIN: (*As he's joined by* ADOLPHO CELIS) We think you might need a little help.

HENRY: (*Pulling out his gun*) This is all the help I need, gentlemen.

(HENRY *pushes* SAM *and the other* CHINESE MAN *past* AUSTIN *and* CELIS *and disappears. Someone runs past carrying a large roast goose. Lights up on* LYDIA *and* ROSA, *who now holds the chest.*)

ROSA: I can't take this!

LYDIA: Hide it in your store. It'll be safe there.

ROSA: Whose is it?

LYDIA: I don't know exactly, but it's certainly not mine.

ROSA: What is it?

LYDIA: I've been afraid to open it.

ROSA: If I'm going to hide it in my store, I want to know what it is.

(ROSA *opens the chest, which is filled gold coins and nuggets.*)

LYDIA: Oooh! Gold!

ROSA: This is worth thousands!

LYDIA: Please take it—please!

ROSA: I can't take it. It belongs to the Chinese, doesn't it?

LYDIA: I can't get caught with it!

ROSA: We have to find a way to give it back!

(*Lights fade on them and come up on* CURLY *and* JOSE MARTINEZ, *30, a Mexican sexton, who are standing above the unseen* CROWD *with* GENE *in between them.* TONG YU *is being held by someone in the darkness of the* CROWD.)

CURLY: We need to have a trial!

VARIOUS: Boo! No trial! Too late for that!

MARTINEZ: ¡Necesitamos tener un juicio! [We need to have a trial!]

CURLY: A quick one! Or it's not justice!

MAN IN CROWD: ¡No hay necesidad de un juzgado! [No need for a trial!]

VARIOUS: Guilty! Hang 'em now! Guilty as charged!

MARTINEZ: ¡Uno rápido! [A quick one!]

(*Suddenly* HENRY *leaps up into view above the unseen* CROWD *but apart from* CURLY, GENE, *and* MARTINEZ.)

HENRY: Listen everybody, have we lost our minds? Cowardly deeds under cover of darkness—!

MAN IN CROWD: *¡No podemos entenderle!* [We can't understand you!]

WOMAN IN CROWD: *¡Vayanse de nuevo a America!* [Go back to America!]

HENRY: *¡Controlense! ¿Que han perdido sus mentes?* [Get ahold of yourselves! Have you all lost your minds?]

MAN IN CROWD: *Habla Espanol!* [He speaks Spanish!]	ANOTHER WOMAN IN CROWD: What's he saying?

HENRY: *¿Que no hay civilizacion en Los Angeles?* [Is there no civilization in Los Angeles?]

CURLY: *("Translating")* Is there no sanitation in Los Angeles?

(The CROWD *laughs.)*

HENRY: *Si no hay justicia para el chino, no hay justicia para cualquier persona.* [If there's no justice for the Chinese, there's no justice for anyone.]

CURLY: You see I have no eyes or parasols!

(Laughter)

HENRY: *¡El mundo nos juzgara por lo que hacemos esta noche!* [The world will judge us for what we do tonight!]

(Lights begin to fade on HENRY *and* CURLY. *Someone runs by laughing carrying bottles of looted wine.)*

CURLY: The whole world knows we're having a great party tonight!

(Laughter. Lights up on TRAFFORD *and* YO HING *in* TRAFFORD'S *cellar. Someone dashes by the* CROWD *with bolts of Chinese silk.)*

YO: Very much thanks, Judge.

TRAFFORD: Mister Hing, you are undoubtedly a criminal and possibly partly responsible for the heinous goings-on this evening, but this is the United States, dammit, and even a criminal has the right not to be dragged out of his home and lynched.

(Sound of gunshots and cheers in the distance.)

YO: Yo Hing no bad. Pay you back. Plenty money. You see.

TRAFFORD: I am ashamed of my city, Mister Hing. Do you know that word: ashamed?

YO: Lose face.

(Lights start to come up on the CROWD, CURLY, GENE, *and* HENRY *again.)*

TRAFFORD: We have all lost face tonight.

HENRY: *Si un crimen ha sido cometido, para eso estan las cortes.* [If a crime has been committed, that is what the courts are for.]

CURLY: Criminy! Let's forget about all this, get a haircut and get laid!

(The unseen CROWD *laughs.)*

HENRY: *¡No ayuda juntar el crimen con otro!* [It does not help to compound the crime with another!]

MAN IN CROWD: Enough Espanol, let's get on with the hanging!

HENRY: No, sir! Not while   CURLY: This is the fun
I'm on watch!   part!

WOMAN IN CROWD: Is he running for office?

ANNOTATION: Henry Hazard was, in fact, elected Mayor of Los Angeles in 1888.

MAN IN CROWD: Stand in our way and you'll get liquidated!

HENRY: *(Pointing his gun)* Go ahead and try it!

(A shot rings out. HENRY *points his gun wildly. Someone grabs* HENRY *and pulls him down.)*

ANOTHER MAN IN CROWD: Stand down, Henry, don't get yourself killed!

*(*HENRY *disappears into the darkness of the* CROWD.*)*

CURLY: Let's get on with this hanging!

MARTINEZ: *¡Es hora de colgar!* [Time for a hanging!]

CURLY: Any last words, heathen?

GENE: Yes.

MARTINEZ: *¡No! ¡Cuelgenlo ya!* [No! Hang him now!]

WOMAN IN CROWD: Enough talking! Hang him!

CURLY: No, the Celestial's earned a final speech!

MAN IN CROWD: Let him speak!

ANOTHER MAN IN CROWD: Let's hear him!

VARIOUS: Yeah! Let's hear what he has to say! Let him explain himself! Shut him up! Let's get this over with!

CURLY: Thank you, good people. *(Gestures to* GENE*)*

GENE: You call me a heathen.

MAN IN CROWD: Ancestor worshipper!

WOMAN IN CROWD: Idolator!

GENE: And I am one proudly.

(Some boos.)

GENE: I have studied Christianity and while the basic faith has some allure, I find myself mystified by the various sects. I looked into Presbyterianism—

(Boos from the CROWD.*)*

GENE: —Only to retreat shudderingly from a belief in a merciless God who had long foreordained most of the helpless human race to an eternal hell.

ANN: Even the heathen know the Presbyterians are wrong!

(Laughter from the unseen crowd)

GENE: Then I dipped into Baptist doctrines—

(CROWD *reaction.)*

GENE: —But found so much warring over the merits of cold-water immersion and the method and time of using it, that I became disgusted with such trivialities.

AUSTIN: The Baptists are all wet!

GENE: Methodism struck me as a thunder-and-lighting religion—all profession and noise.

WOMAN IN CROWD: But they got great hymns!

GENE: The Congregationalists deterred me with their starchiness and self-conscious true-goodness, and their desire only for high-toned affiliates.

MAN IN CROWD: Snobs! They're a bunch of snobs!

GENE: Unitarianism seemed all doubt, doubting even itself. But all Protestant sects are certain of one thing, and that is their united hatred of Catholicism, which has returned with interest this animosity. It haughtily declares itself the only true Church, outside of which there is no salvation. And that its chief prelate is the personal representative of God on earth, and that he is infallible.

ANNOTATION: If you're thinking this an unlikely speech from a man threatened by a lynch mob, you are correct. These thoughts come from an 1887 essay by Wong Chin Foo entitled *Why Am I a Heathen?* Gene Tong begged for his life in fluent English and Spanish but in reality was pried away from his wife's arms—

TONG YU: *(Rushing into the light)* Chee! *Mm-ho bay kuoy day dai-ngor-jiao!* [Don't let them take me!]

(The CROWD *quickly pulls* TONG YU *back into the darkness.)*

ANNOTATION: —Without time for such eloquence.

GENE: So if I find it hard to turn the other cheek—

CURLY: Enough of this preaching!

*(*CURLY *shoots* GENE *in the mouth, killing him instantly.* TONG YU *screams and is spirited away still screaming.* SISTER PRUDENCIA, *who has been watching silently, runs away in horror. The* CROWD, *still stunned by* GENE'S *eloquence, hesitates for a moment before bursting into a half-hearted cheer.)*

CURLY: Wonder if he's got any money on him.

VARIOUS: Get his money! He's a rich doctor! Gotta be something there! *¡Este tenía arta lana!*

GEORGE: *(Jumping up to grab* GENE's *right hand)* And look—a diamond ring! *(Tries to loosen it. Gets out a knife)* This ring's on tight!

VARIOUS: Leave him alone! He's already dead! Cut it off! Cut it off! We wasted too much time already on this one!

*(*GEORGE *succeeds in severing the bloody pinky finger with the ring on it, displaying it for the* CROWD. *Again, some cheers, but not universal acclaim.)*

GEORGE: Got it!

*(*GEORGE *pulls the ring from the finger and puts it in his pocket.* LEE TONG *suddenly bursts from behind the* CROWD, *jumping up beside* GEORGE, *waving his gun.)*

LEE TONG: No—hurt—brother!

YUT HO: *(Bursting from the* CROWD *into the light)* *Lee Tong, mm-ho gum-swoi.* [Lee Tong, don't be a sentimental fool!]

(LEE TONG'S gun goes off but ill-aimed. At the same time GEORGE and CURLY knock LEE TONG into the CROWD, falling on top of him. The CROWD pulls YUT HO back into the darkness as they did TONG YU.)

CURLY: Get him, George!   GEORGE: Get his gun!

(BIDDY appears and tries to pull YUT HO out of the crowd to safety, but YUT HO pulls away from her.)

VARIOUS: Shoot him! He's got a gun! Was that his brother? Is that his wife? Don't let him get away! ¡Matenlo!

YUT HO: *Ho-choi yao-lay. Nguor day on-cheung-nah!* [Now we're both caught, thanks to you. We were safe!]

(LEE TONG is hauled to his feet by GEORGE and CURLY grabs YUT HO.)

LEE TONG: *Oi-nguor yew tsai-chee kuoy-day, kuoy high nguor geh hing-dai!* [I had to stop them. He's my brother!]

YUT HO: *Lay mo joe-dough. Yee-qing tai chee-lah.* [No you didn't. It was too late.]

CURLY: What shall we do with these two?

VARIOUS: Hang 'em like his brother! They're all the same! Shoot him! Hang 'em both!

GEORGE: I got special plans for this one.

CURLY: I'll take charge of the lady.

BURNS: *(Appears, wielding a gun)* What are you doing with that lady, Curly?

CURLY: Taking her to jail for her own safety.

BURNS: See that you do. George?

GEORGE: James.

BURNS: Did I just see you mutilate a corpse?

GEORGE: Not at all, James.

(*Everyone freezes, while* GEORGE, *without* BURNS *seeing, slips the severed finger into* CURLY's *pocket.*)

LEE: (*In 1891*) That's how you got the finger?

REVEREND CRENSHAW: (*In 1891*) I didn't cut him!

LEE: No, just shot him. And discovered your talent for preaching to the ignorant.

(*Everyone unfreezes.*)

BIDDY: I saw it, too. You done cut off that man's finger.

(*Silence for a moment*)

GEORGE: Frank, whose word you gonna take? A city councilman or a nigress used to be owned body and soul by Robert Smith?

(*Another moment of silence*)

BURNS: What's your plan with that boy?

GEORGE: To jail as well, I suppose.

(*Sounds of guns and screams in the distance. The unseen* CROWD *reacts.*)

VARIOUS: More of 'em! Up to more no good! Probably shot more white folks! Let's go get 'em! ¡*Vamos a Cogerlos!*

BURNS: If I don't find him in jail tomorrow, I'll have your office, George!

(BURNS *rushes off into the darkness, as the unseen* CROWD *absorbs* CURLY *with* YUT HO. *Some of the* CROWD *take chairs with with them, set them in orderly rows, and seat themselves.*)

YUT HO: Lee Tong!   LEE TONG: *Nguor woi wan-nay, Yut Ho!* [I'll find you, Yut Ho!]

GEORGE: You watch yourself, Biddy Mason.

BIDDY: I'm watching you, Mister Fall.

GEORGE: Tonight's the Chinese, but the Vigilance Committee took care of a Frenchman last year, and some Mexicans before that.

BIDDY: You best be taking that nice man to jail, Mr. Fall, or Sheriff Burns'll take care of you.

(ROSA *appears with* HILLIARD.)

ROSA: There they are, Hilliard.

HILLIARD: Mister Fall, where are you taking that boy?

GEORGE: To jail! For the millionth time!

HILLIARD: I'll be happy to escort him for you.

GEORGE: I promised the Sheriff.

HILLIARD: *(Raising two pistols)* Councilman Fall, I may be better qualified. This is a Pepper Box Revolver produced by T & W Harrison, who specialized in the manufacture of pepper box pistols during the period 1840 to 1860. It was one of the first to self cock the hammer and rotate the cylinder by the single act of pulling the trigger.

GEORGE: Are you threatening me, Mister Loewenberg?

BIDDY, HILLIARD, ROSA: Loewenstein.

HILLIARD: This is a German smoothbore pocket pistol, newly arrived from Europe. I haven't had a chance to test it yet, but I understand it has a tendency to go off on its own.

GEORGE: *(Releasing* LEE TONG) Mister Loewenstern, you leave me no choice but to report you to the city council for violating our ordinance against weaponry of foreign manufacture.

ANNOTATION: There was no such ordinance.

HILLIARD: Why don't you move along now, before one of these pistols malfunctions in your direction?

(GEORGE *disappears.* LEE TONG *almost collapses with relief.*)

ROSA: *(Cutting his bonds)* You are Gene Tong's brother?

LEE TONG: Yes. Brother—he *was*— *(He is overwhelmed.)*

HILLIARD: Come to our store—you'll be safe.

LEE TONG: My—wife—! He take!

ROSA: You must save yourself!

LEE TONG: Must to save her!

HILLIARD: You'll get yourself killed.

ROSA: Maybe he'll spare her because she's a woman.

LEE TONG: No! He—hurt—!

BIDDY: There's no stopping him. He gotta at least try.

HILLIARD: *(Handing* LEE TONG *one of the guns)* Very well, go. We'll be at the store.

ROSA: Curly Crenshaw works at the stable on Temple. Try there.

LEE TONG: *(Bows)* Thank you. But—why to help?

HILLIARD: We know a pogrom when we see one.

(LEE TONG *runs off.*)

ROSA: Biddy, come. I've got something to show you.

(Lights fade on ROSA, HILLIARD *and* BIDDY *as they join the others in the rows of chairs. Lights up on* CURLY *and* YUT HO *in a stable. He is standing. She sits, looking relaxed, on a hay bale.)*

YUT HO: You save me.

CURLY: It's your men that's the problem. None of this woulda happened but for them tong highbinders getting in a shoot out. You're innocent, surely.

YUT HO: Inno-cent.

CURLY: You're safe here in the barn. I work— *(Gestures, awkwardly)* —Here. Groom for the horses.

YUT HO: Safe?

CURLY: We're far enough from Nigger Alley, no one'd think to look—

YUT HO: Sit. *(She pats the bale.)*

CURLY: No, I better—

YUT HO: Me scared. Sit.

CURLY: Well, all right. *(Sits)* You're the real victim in all this. Passed back and forth between companies like a sack of flour, traded—

(CURLY stops as YUT HO begins to stroke his hair.)

CURLY: Miss...you're married. I know you're married.

YUT HO: To a boy. You man.

CURLY: Look, I'm glad I can be of help, but—

YUT HO: Hold.

CURLY: What? I—

YUT HO: Hold!

(YUT HO grabs CURLY. After a tentative moment they kiss. Then recline on the hay bale.)

LEE: *(Appearing in 1891)* Reverend Crenshaw.

REVEREND CRENSHAW: *(Sitting up in 1891)* Sir?

LEE: The Chinese woman seduced you?

REVEREND CRENSHAW: I figured twas natural. I'd saved her from certain death. Bold, but natural.

LEE: Out of...gratitude?

REVEREND CRENSHAW: She was most grateful.

LEE: *(Tense)* I heard differently, sir.

REVEREND CRENSHAW: How? Only the two of us were present. That my rendition might differ from the truth interests me greatly. Who is your source?

ANNOTATION: In fact, at his trial on February 17, 1872, Curly Crenshaw testified that he'd taken custody of a Chinese woman that night but couldn't remember what he'd done with her.

(Sudden lighting change thrusts CURLY *back into 1871 and into the middle of his rape of* YUT HO. *She struggles and screams, but it's evident that she's somehow restrained, perhaps tied to the hay bale.)*

CURLY: *(As he thrusts)* Mongol bitch! Too good for regular fellows, catering to the carriage trade—taste *this!*

*(*YUT HO *screams in pain.)*

CURLY: Shut up! *(Shoves gun against her head)* You're as good to fuck dead as alive!

*(*YUT HO *wills herself to complete passivity, as if suddenly dead.* CURLY *withdraws and backs away from her, doing up his trousers. Slowly, she begins to smile at him.)*

CURLY: *(Notices her smile)* What?

YUT HO: Poison.

CURLY: What?

YUT HO: I am poison.

*(*YUT HO *smiles more broadly, maliciously, and* CURLY *looks more frightened and confused.)*

CURLY: What?

*(*LEE TONG *appears, aiming the gun at* CURLY.*)*

LEE TONG: Let go.

CURLY: *(Seeing him)* What?

LEE TONG: Let go gun.

YUT HO: *Lee Tong! Yee qing tai-chee lah.* [Lee Tong! You are too late.]

(CURLY *drops the gun.* LEE TONG *picks it up.)*

LEE TONG: *Tai chee?* [Too late for what?]

CURLY: Speak English! This is America!

LEE TONG: *(Gesturing with gun)* Let go wife.

(CURLY *unties* YUT HO's *bonds and she sits up.)*

CURLY: Take her. She's no good, anyways.

(YUT HO *goes to* LEE TONG, *but does not embrace him.)*

LEE TONG: Me kill now.

YUT HO: *Mm-ho-ah!* [No, don't!]	CURLY: I didn't do anything!
LEE TONG: *Deem-gai-ah? Kyou seung hoy juor lay. Nguor you sat say kuoy.* [Why not? He hurt you, didn't he? I have to kill him.]	CURLY: Whatever she says, she's lying! I didn't touch her!

YUT HO: *Nguor yee-qing sat juor kuoy.* [I already have.]

LEE TONG: *(After a moment)* I turn...other cheek.

(Lighting change puts YUT HO *in the dark and relocates* LEE *and* REVEREND CRENSHAW *in 1891.)*

REVEREND CRENSHAW: What did you say?

LEE: I turned the other cheek.

REVEREND CRENSHAW: You?

LEE: I've told you no lies, Reverend. Would that you returned the favor. I am a bone collector. I've come to collect— *(Gestures to the finger)* —My brother's bones.

REVEREND CRENSHAW: Your brother?

LEE: He saved my life. I'm here to save his soul.

REVEREND CRENSHAW: You're the husband.

LEE: Would you like to know what became of the wife?

REVEREND CRENSHAW: Not especially. Why would I?

LEE: She lived almost nine more years.

(YUT HO, *much changed, unwell, appears, illustrating what* LEE *describes.*)

LEE: For the last two years, she was blind. At the very end, demented. I saw it coming earlier when she couldn't remember every day words. When she developed an odd gait.

(YUT HO *finds her way to the hay bale and lies down as on a sick bed.* LEE *goes to her.*)

LEE: She became helpless. Entirely in my hands.

YUT HO: Lee Tong?

LEE: Yes?

YUT HO: My bones...

LEE: Your bones?

YUT HO: To China.

LEE: Of course.

YUT HO: I miss it. That is my sickness. Can you give me your brother's cure?

LEE: (*Produces a cup of water*) China in a cup. (*Sprinkles dust in it.*)

(*They smile.* YUT HO *drinks.*)

REVEREND CRENSHAW: Blind?

LEE: Syphilitic. Like all the girls from green mansions.

YUT HO: I'm going home.

(*Lights fade on* YUT HO *as* LEE *rejoins* REVEREND CRENSHAW.*)

REVEREND CRENSHAW: But that's not the end.

LEE: It was for me.

REVEREND CRENSHAW: You couldn't *love* her. Her body—

LEE: You Christians preach love, Reverend, but know nothing about it.

REVEREND CRENSHAW: Why've you come?

LEE: For a funeral. *(Gesturing toward the finger)* And this.

REVEREND CRENSHAW: That's all?

LEE: And for your words. *(Pulls out gun from previous scene)* Christians make a ritual of confession, do they not? It's almost beautiful.

REVEREND CRENSHAW: I haven't told you everything.

LEE: You've told me enough.

REVEREND CRENSHAW: And there's more you haven't told me.

LEE: You know the facts of the matter better than I. Eighteen Chinese men and one boy were shot or hung that night, ten percent of the Chinese population.

ANNOTATION: In 1880, poet-historian A J Wilson said the "American 'hoodlum' and Mexican 'greaser,' Irish 'tramp' and French 'communist' —all joined to murder and dispatch the foe. He who did not shoot, could shout; he who feared to stab, could steal; there was work for all."

LEE: One hundred fifty people were named as participants.

ANNOTATION: But the list has since been lost. And the newspapers agreed the actual number was more than five hundred, with individual identities disguised by darkness and dissembling.

LEE: There was public outrage.

ANNOTATION: An editorial published in the Los Angeles Star on May 9th, 1872, entitled "An Ineffectual

Police Force," reads: "The incompetency of our police force has so often been demonstrated that it no longer remains questionable to anyone. There are probably men employed on the force who desire to do their duty as public officers in all occasions, but as a whole, the organization is rotten from head to foot and wants to undergo a thorough cleansing."

LEE: Twenty-one men were indicted and nine convicted of manslaughter in the death of Gene Tong.

ANNOTATION: One witness, Benjamin McLaughlin—

(Lights up on MCLAUGHLIN.*)*

ANNOTATION: —Implicated Crenshaw by testifying that—

MCLAUGHLIN: Curly was there. He said he'd killed three—he talked considerable about shooting Chinamen for some time.

REVEREND CRENSHAW: The convictions were overturned a year later!

LEE: Because the prosecution failed to prove my brother was actually murdered. *(With the finger)* This seems proof enough for me. But who has the ring?

REVEREND CRENSHAW: George Fall, I told you.

LEE: What became of him?

REVEREND CRENSHAW: I heard he died of the typhoid in Nevada.

LEE: *(Producing the ring)* Typhoid. Hmm.

REVEREND CRENSHAW: For whose funeral have you come, sir?

LEE: Which reminds me. One more thing did happen that night.

(Lights come up on YUT HO *lying down on the hay bale with* BIDDY *tending her and* LEE *becomes* LEE TONG *standing apart.)*

REVEREND CRENSHAW: Whose funeral?!

LEE TONG: Why you come?

BIDDY: I been paid.

LEE TONG: Who pay? Yo Hing?

BIDDY: Mrs Loewenstein. I wouldn't be here otherwise.

LEE TONG: Yut Ho—hurt?

BIDDY: She'll be all right. *(Handing* YUT HO *a cup)* As soon as she drinks this.

YUT HO: What is, please?

BIDDY: Think of it as insurance. You know that word?

LEE TONG & YUT HO: No.

YUT HO: What is?

BIDDY: I'd call it ground up bugs, but I think you call it *ban mao*.

LEE TONG: *Ban mao!*

YUT HO: *Mm-gan yew, Lee Tong. Nguor high-yew yum gah.* [It's all right, Lee Tong. I have to take it.]

LEE TONG: *Ho long.* [It's   BIDDY: Powerful Chinese
very strong!]   medicine. From Gene
                                    Tong.

YUT HO: *Nguor yew yeung-ching ching-choi kuoy.* [I need to clean him from me inside and out.]

LEE TONG: No—maybe hurt!

YUT HO: *(To* BIDDY*)* From Gene Tong?

*(*BIDDY *nods.* YUT HO *turns to* LEE TONG*.)*

BIDDY: I'm a patient woman by nature. I can wait. *(After a moment)* But not forever.

(YUT HO *drinks.*)

YUT HO: *(Indicating herself)* No med-cine strong enough.

BIDDY: You are so right, child. But with God's help we do what we can. *(To* LEE TONG*)* Take her away. Los Angeles ain't safe for you. Take what is yours and go.

LEE TONG: What is mine?

BIDDY: *(Leaving)* And keep her warm.

LEE TONG: Warm?

BIDDY: Warm—

(BIDDY *embraces* LEE TONG. *He flinches but accepts the embrace.*)

BIDDY: Hold her to keep her warm.

LEE TONG: *(Whispering)* Her no like.

BIDDY: She may not like it, but she needs it.

(For a moment LEE TONG *and* YUT HO *stare at each other from a distance, then he approaches her carefully. Suddenly, she clutches her stomach with one hand as the ban mao begins to take effect.)*

YUT HO: *(Raising her other arm)* Need.

(LEE TONG *embraces* YUT HO.)

YUT HO: Like.

(As they embrace, they dislodge the chest of gold, which had been hidden next to YUT HO *on the hay bale. The gold spills out. They look at the gold, at each other, then to* BIDDY, *but she is gone, having joined the others in the rows of chairs.)*

ANNOTATION: Biddy Mason passed from this life January 15, 1891 and was laid to rest in Evergreen cemetery in Los Angeles, but her grave remained unmarked until Mayor Tom Bradley and three thousand members of the First African Methodist

Episcopal Church unveiled a tombstone and declared November 16, 1989 Biddy Mason Day.

(Lights out on YUT HO *as* LEE *rejoins* REVEREND CRENSHAW *in 1891.)*

REVEREND CRENSHAW: That's whose funeral.

LEE: Perhaps. *(Puts the final gold piece in* REVEREND CRENSHAW's *hand.)* You've earned this.

REVEREND CRENSHAW: I'm raising my price.

LEE: I agree—a higher price must be paid. *(Audibly plays with the gun)* You know a little bit about guns, Reverend. What about a trade for that finger? This Pepper Box Revolver is by now at least forty years old, very nearly antique, and undoubtedly worth more than fifty dollars. Self-cocking and rotating— I've kept it in working order.

REVEREND CRENSHAW: I'm not the same man.

LEE: Court records and newspaper accounts from twenty years ago give Curly Crenshaw's real name as either L F Crenshaw—

ANNOTATION: *People vs L F Crenshaw et al,* Case 1084, dated December 2, 1871, District Court, Los Angeles County Court Records.

LEE: A L Crenshaw—

ANNOTATION: *Los Angeles Star,* October 26th, 1871.

LEE: Or A F Crenshaw—

ANNOTATION: Since being here, his associations have been of the lowest character. His favorite resort was a rendezvous of low women, pick-pockets, and cutthroats. *The Los Angeles Daily News,* February 20th, 1872.

LEE: And you appear in census records under no name whatsoever. But I recognize you, Reverend, and your own words condemn you.

REVEREND CRENSHAW: I meant that I've changed.

LEE: No, but I have. I am a doctor. I speak English. I am my brother. American.

REVEREND CRENSHAW: Look at me!

LEE: You're blind, syphilitic, and possibly demented. Perhaps I'm only a figment of your diseased and guilty imagination bringing justice twenty years late.

ANNOTATION: Lee Tong, did not, in fact, exist. Census records show the physician Gene Tong had a younger brother, but the name is incorrectly recorded gibberish. Court documents indicate Yut Ho's husband was named Lee Yong. The brother and the husband were most certainly not the same person.

REVEREND CRENSHAW: There is justice, sir, and there is mercy.

LEE: Mercy. A Christian concept. But I'm a heathen.

REVEREND CRENSHAW: I appeal to your morality apart from any religion.

LEE: You're asking me to once again turn the other cheek. Then I was Chinese. Now I'm American. My brother would be proud of me at last.

REVEREND CRENSHAW: What will you do, sir?

LEE: What will you do, Reverend?

REVEREND CRENSHAW: Whatever you ask.

LEE: My brother's finger lies before you. Pick it up.

(REVEREND CRENSHAW *hesitates*.)

LEE: These Pepper Box Revolvers have the strange quirk of occasionally discharging all the chambers at once, which is awkward but effective.

(REVEREND CRENSHAW *picks up the finger.*)

LEE: Now put it in your mouth.

REVEREND CRENSHAW: What?

LEE: I thought you liked the taste of justice.

REVEREND CRENSHAW: The moisture will destroy it.

LEE: Or is it mercy on my part?

REVEREND CRENSHAW: The flesh—

LEE: *(Spinning the cylinder)* The dried meat softening
as your saliva revivifies dead tissue. The thirsty skin
swelling like a sausage on your tongue. Cells breaking
off, floating inside your mouth, making their way into
your body, becoming part of you. History becoming
part of you—whatever lies you've told, whatever
inaccuracies have been recorded, this will be a fact:
flesh in your mouth.

REVEREND CRENSHAW: Have you no respect?

LEE: I'm a patient man, Reverend Crenshaw. *(No
response)* L F, A L, A F, Curly. I wonder whether you
yourself exist, with no census record, conflicting
accounts of your name. Will your grave be unmarked?

REVEREND CRENSHAW: Don't...

LEE: You've eluded history, Reverend. Disappeared
already. But what good's history? Unreliable.
Conflated. Conflicting. Edited.

REVEREND CRENSHAW: History is past—

(In dim light, the CROWD *appears seated in the twelve chairs
arranged in three rows of four.* YUT HO *has joined them.)*

ANNOTATION: In the San Francisco newspaper, *Alta
California*, on October 26th, 1871, there was speculation
that the people of Los Angeles—

ALL: Sickened with last night's horrors, are determined that no stigma of like character shall ever again rest upon us.

LEE: Truly past, Reverend?

SANCHEZ: *(Appearing in a zoot suit)* 1943.

REVEREND CRENSHAW: Yes! The rule of law—

(REVEREND CRENSHAW stumbles blindly into the audience, a frightening break in the fourth wall. He moves so unsteadily, LEE does not run after him, but pursues him at a steady walk.)

BIDDY: *(Appearing dressed in clothes from 1965)* 1965.

REVEREND CRENSHAW: And we're still changing. Not crystalized—

LEE: Are we?

(TONG YU appears dressed as a Korean shop owner, circa 1992, holding a rifle.)

TONG YU: 1992.

ANNOTATION: Or just becoming more...American?

LEE: *(Spins the cylinder)* You hold the answer in your hand. Plenty of time to decide what to do. No rush to judgment. *(Spins the cylinder)* I can wait.

SANCHEZ: *Puedo esperar.* [I can wait.]

BIDDY: I can wait.

TONG YU: *Gee dahl ee gae.* [I can wait.]

LEE: *(Spins the cylinder)* I can wait.

END OF PLAY

ALTERNATIVE ENDING #1

LEE: Truly past, Reverend?

(SANCHEZ *appears in a zoot suit.*)

REVEREND CRENSHAW: Yes! The rule of law—

(BIDDY *appears dressed in clothes from 1965.* REVEREND CRENSHAW *stumbles blindly into the audience, a frightening break in the fourth wall. He moves so unsteadily,* LEE *does not run after him, but pursues him at a steady walk.*)

REVEREND CRENSHAW: And we're still changing. Not crystalized—

LEE: Are we?

(TONG YU *appears dressed as a Korean shop owner, circa 1992, holding a rifle.*)

ANNOTATION: Or just becoming more...American?

LEE: *(Spins the cylinder)* You hold the answer in your hand. Plenty of time to decide what to do. No rush to judgment. *(Spins the cylinder)* I can wait.

SANCHEZ: *Puedo esperar.* [I can wait.]

BIDDY: I can wait.

TONG YU: *Gee dahl ee gae.* [I can wait.]

LEE: *(Spins the cylinder)* I can wait.

END OF PLAY

ALTERNATIVE ENDING #2

LEE: Truly past, Reverend?

(REVEREND CRENSHAW *stumbles blindly into the audience,
a frightening break in the fourth wall. He moves so
unsteadily,* LEE *does not run after him, but pursues him at a
steady walk.*)

REVEREND CRENSHAW: Yes! The rule of law—and we're
still changing. Not crystalized—

LEE: Are we?

ANNOTATION: Or just becoming more...American?

LEE: *(Spins the cylinder)* You hold the answer in your
hand. Plenty of time to decide what to do. No rush
to judgment. *(Spins the cylinder)* I can wait. *(Spins the
cylinder)* I can wait.

END OF PLAY

www.ingramcontent.com/pod-product-compliance
Lightning Source LLC
Chambersburg PA
CBHW052157090426
42741CB00010B/2304